Closing Chapters

Reminiscences of a Hospice Nurse

Closing Chapters

*Reminiscences of a
Hospice Nurse*

Joan Stempel, MSN, RN

Cover art and design by

Danielle Egnew

The names of many individuals in this book have been changed.

INTRODUCTION

I spent a large part of my thirty-year nursing career working with terminally ill people and their loved ones as either a hospice nurse or a community case manager. During this time, I experienced a medical revolution in the way dying individuals are treated. When I entered nurses training in the late fifties, my first assignment was working on the medical floor of a hospital, caring for people who had chronic conditions such as heart disease, diabetes or lung problems. People who were dying were also admitted to this area. Whenever possible, rooms were assigned to patients according to the amount of nursing care they needed. Patients who were seriously ill but expected to recover were placed nearest the nurses' station. Medical staff felt there was little they could do for dying patients beyond taking care of their personal needs: bathing, turning, pain medication and occasional bites of food or sips of water. Since these individuals needed minimal care, it seemed logical to assign them rooms at the end of the corridor, as far from the nurses' station as possible.

These patients received pain medication on a strict every four-hour schedule regardless of the amount of pain the person was experiencing. Doctors feared an overdose of a narcotic might cause someone to stop breathing and hasten the individual's death, or that the patient would become addicted. Physicians would occasionally glance in on a dying patient and say hello to the family, but rarely took the time to talk to them or answer any questions. Sadly, many people died alone and in pain.

I was very uncomfortable whenever I was assigned to care for someone who was dying. I sensed that the patient and family had needs that weren't being addressed by the medical staff but had no idea what those needs were, let alone how to meet them. When three of my patients died in one week during my second month of training, I was ready to quit nursing. I couldn't stand seeing people neglected and suffering. I felt useless. Little did I know that I would spend much of my professional and personal life involved with end-of-life care.

During this time, I had my first personal experience of losing someone close to me. Two girls in my nursing class, along with three other young people, were killed in an auto accident involving a drunk driver. One of the girls, Janette, I had known since first grade. I'll never forget visiting Janette's mother shortly before her daughter's funeral and witnessing first-hand the heartbreak that comes from losing a child. Because our nursing class was small, only 14 girls, we were a close-knit group. Losing two of our classmates hit us especially hard. Looking back, it seems incredible we were not offered any type of grief counseling. Instead, we supported one another as best we could and muddled through the next three years. I remember feeling absolutely numb for months after those deaths. I was just nineteen.

Difficult as that experience was, going through it helped me begin to understand the emotional turmoil one goes through when someone you care about dies- a lesson I was able to use later when I began my hospice work.

I graduated from nursing, worked several years as a surgical nurse, then married and had two children. I put my nursing career on hold for a few years and concentrated instead on raising my two young daughters. But despite my temporary retirement from the workplace, family and friends turned to me for support and medical advice. During this time the husbands of my two best friends each developed cancer and died within six weeks of one another. They were both 41. The story of one of these couples, Dan and Beth, describes this difficult time.

Early in the seventies, Elizabeth Kubler-Ross's work on the emotional stages of grief, along with the work of Dame Cicely Saunders at St. Christopher's Hospice in England, began to be published. Groups dedicated to creating hospices in this country like St. Christopher's began to spring up across the United States. "Death with dignity" became a rallying cry.

The first hospice in this country opened in New Haven, Connecticut in 1974. Soon other hospice programs began appearing across the country, supported by grants or funds raised by private individuals. There was little opposition from the AMA to the hospice movement, as most doctors at that time were content to let someone else care for their dying patients. In 1982 Congress passed a bill that allowed hospice care to be covered by Medicare. Many private medical insurance companies soon followed Congress' lead.

Since this field of medicine was new to nurses and doctors in this country, there was little formal training available for hospice workers. We gathered much of our understanding of the management of symptoms, especially pain, from work that had been done in hospices in England. Knowledge about ways to provide the emotional and spiritual support needed by dying individuals and their families grew as hospice workers learned from working with these individuals. Information gained in this way was shared among professionals through conferences, workshops and professional journals.

Hospice seemed like a natural fit for me. I was finally able to provide dying patients and those close to them the kind of supportive care I had instinctively known they needed. What a change from those early student days. Gone were the feelings of frustration and guilt, replaced by feelings of gratitude that I now had the necessary knowledge needed to keep the dying comfortable, and with the help of other hospice team members, provide the spiritual and emotional support that was so badly needed.

During my hospice years, one of my jobs was the orientation of new staff. I found it was a challenge for medical personnel, especially nurses, to change the focus of their care from improving the health of patients and curing their diseases to palliative care with its emphasis on managing physical symptoms and addressing emotional and spiritual needs. One of the most effective teaching tools I found to help staff make this transition was sharing people's stories. Using stories in this way allowed new staff members to observe the individual's and family's process and to experience first-hand the emotional and spiritual challenges which can occur. I have used this same technique to share the knowledge I have gained from working with patients, friends and family members as they faced the final chapters of their lives. Each story highlights a different part of the dying process and one begins to see how each person and family handle death in their own unique way. These stories relate some of the challenges that occurred and how they were met, not only with strength but also with humor. Many questions people ask are addressed in these stories, such as: How do you provide emotional support to dying individuals and their grieving loved ones? What words can you use when saying goodbye to someone you care about and how do you give them permission to die? What are ways I can teach my children about death? How does my "death history" affect my ability to be a caregiver? Why are Advanced Directives important? My hope is that this book will not only be of help to those who work with terminally ill individuals but also to anyone interested in learning more about this final part of life. The more we understand this process, the better equipped we will be to make end-of-life decisions not only for ourselves but also for our friends and family.

JANET

People die the same way they lived.

The phone rang just as I was walking out the door to join friends for lunch. I ignored the persistent ringing and kept walking. As my hand reached for the doorknob, the answering machine came on. I heard my friend Janet's voice leaving me a message. I ran back and picked up the phone. "I'm here, Janet," I said, slightly out of breath from running. "What a nice surprise. How are you?" There was a slight hesitation in Janet's voice. "Actually, that's why I'm calling you. I might need your help."

Janet was one of my oldest and dearest friends. She had grown up in the Midwest, the youngest of four children and the only girl. Her father, a German with strict rules about how children should behave, was principal of the local grade school. Rule number one in his household was children were never to complain or show emotion. For instance, when Janet came running home from school one afternoon with skinned elbows and knees after falling off her bike, the first question she was asked was not "Are you hurt?" but rather "Did you cry?"

I had also grown up in a family of three boys. Unlike Janet, I was the oldest rather than the youngest. Janet and I often joked through the years that we were the sisters we both desperately wanted, growing up in those male-dominated families.

We both moved to the San Francisco Bay area shortly after we graduated with our degrees in nursing, Janet from a university in Wisconsin, I from one in Montana, my home state. The two of us met when we started working at the same hospital. When Janet and her friend Carla suddenly found they needed to replace a roommate, they invited me to move in with them. I eagerly agreed.

Janet and I were typical women of the sixties. We married and had children, two girls and a boy for Janet, two girls for me. Because we had no family nearby, we became each other's family. We helped one another

1

over the rough spots, Janet losing her parents to cancer, me dealing with several miscarriages and eventually my mother-in-law with Alzheimer's. Through the years our families went camping and houseboating together and often shared holidays. Our kids grew up feeling more like cousins than family friends.

By the early eighties the hustle and bustle of the Bay area began to wear on all of us. Janet and her husband Roger moved with their family to Oregon, while my husband and I headed to Arizona, where I began working as a hospice home care nurse at a local hospital.

Now, as I stood holding the phone something in Janet's tone caught my attention. "What's the matter, Janet. Is everything all right? Did something happen? Are Roger and the kids okay?"

It seemed like an eternity before Janet answered. I heard her take a deep breath and say in her matter-of- fact-voice, "Oh, Joan, I don't know how to tell you this. I've just gotten the most horrible news you can imagine. I have pancreatic cancer."

"Wow." I was stunned, not wanting to believe what I was hearing. Being nurses, we both knew that unless something miraculous happened, Janet had just received a death sentence. She was only 57. My age. "Oh Janet, I don't know what to say. I am so sorry. How awful for you, for all of you." I could feel my eyes brimming with tears. "I am so sorry you have to go through this. What can I do? What do you need?"

We talked for a while. Janet explained that Roger was having a difficult time and was unable to talk about her illness without crying. The kids were rallying around, providing all the help she needed for the moment.

"What can I do, Janet? Anything you need, I will do it." "What I need from you right now is your expertise," Janet said. "I need you to help me figure out the best way to handle all of this."

A week later I was on a plane to Oregon. I wanted some time with Janet while she was still strong enough to enjoy a visit. We had lots to talk about.

Janet had started chemotherapy the week I arrived. She knew the likelihood of a cure with her type of cancer was slim, but she was hoping to buy herself a little more time. As the result of the chemotherapy, Janet had little appetite and was beginning to lose her hair. She had become very weak and found walking even short distances difficult. Janet was on a regular regimen of pain medication and had lost considerable weight. When I saw her, I wanted to put my arms around her and cry, something I knew she would hate.

Soon after my arrival we made a list of things Janet wanted to accomplish while I was there. The number-one thing on her list was buying a wig. She said she wanted something short and close to her own hair color. "Would you buy it for me?" she asked. "I know if I send Roger to the store, he will come back with something long, blond and flowing." We laughed, knowing that is exactly the look Roger would go for.

The week flew by. We figured out a diet that felt good on Janet's sensitive stomach. We got a wheelchair from the local loan chest so Roger could take her on outings, something they both enjoyed. We met and talked to the local hospice nurse who would be caring for Janet and we learned about their program. Janet wanted to stay at home throughout her illness, if Roger and the kids could somehow manage her care. I promised that when the end drew close, I would be there to help. "I'm not about to let you go off anywhere without being there to wave goodbye," I gently teased her.

Not all my visit was spent on business. We often sat reminiscing over cups of tea about all the good times we'd had through the years. When we traded stories about how great our kids and grandchildren were, Janet would look at me and give me a satisfied smile, saying, "We did good, Joanie, we did good."

Janet was feeling stronger when it came time for me to leave. She rode with us to the airport, sitting in the front seat beside her husband. As we pulled into the lane for departing flights the thought suddenly struck me, this could be the last time I would ever see Janet. Filled with a sudden rush of grief, I reached over and put my hand on Janet's shoulder and gently squeezed it. "Bye, Janet. I love you," I said as I started getting out of the car. I waited for a response, but Janet just sat there staring straight ahead. I thought, "Maybe she didn't hear me," so I repeated the words a little louder. "Bye Janet. I love you." Still no response, but I noticed Janet's back become a little more rigid, as she continued to sit there silent, not turning around, refusing to look at me or acknowledge what I had said. Then I got it. Janet was sticking to the family rules. My dear friend knew if she turned around and faced me, she would start crying. She had lived 57 years without breaking the no-crying rule and she was not about to start breaking it now. I slowly got out of the car and began walking into the airport. As I reached the door, I turned around for a last look. Janet continued to sit staring straight ahead as the car slowly drove out of sight.

The phone call I had been dreading came four months later, on Memorial Day weekend, while my husband and I were visiting friends in San Diego. Janet's son Mitch called to say Janet had suddenly become much weaker and could no longer get out of bed. Although the hospice nurse was coming daily, her family was finding it difficult to care for her. They needed help. Could I come?

I arrived the next day to find Janet resting in a hospital bed. The bed was set up in the living room where she could look out the windows at her rose garden. Because she was so weak, talking had become a real effort for her. I walked to her bedside and took her hand, squeezing it gently. "Janet, I'm here," I said. Janet opened her eyes briefly and smiled. "Thank you for coming." Her eyes closed, I could see her relax and let go as though a great weight had been lifted. Those were her last words; by morning she had slipped into a coma.

The family gathered at her bedside and the waiting began. Janet's daughters Lucy and Jenny stayed with us during the day, returning to their nearby homes at night to be with their own families. Mitch, who had come from California, stayed 24/7 and helped with Janet's physical care. It was a difficult time emotionally for all of us.

Although people in a coma appear unresponsive, they are still able to hear what is said to them. Knowing this, I encouraged Janet's children to continue talking to her, and to say their goodbyes. One afternoon, as Lucy and I were sitting in the rose garden talking, Lucy said, "Last night, I got to thinking about what you said about Mom still being able to hear and I decided to write her a letter. I want to make sure she knows how much I loved having her for a mother and how much I am going to miss her." Tears began to fill her eyes. "Would you read my letter to Mom for me? Sometime when I'm not here? I know if I try to read it to her, I would cry so hard I couldn't talk." I took the letter from Lucy and slipped it into my pocket, giving her a hug. "I'll do it tonight," I said.

Later that night when we were alone, I sat with Janet and read Lucy's touching goodbye. Although Janet didn't open her eyes, there was a feeling of alertness about her and I knew she was listening closely to every word. Thank goodness, there are no rules about crying in my family!

The days passed slowly, and we began to look for ways to fill the time. The girls helped me make the spaghetti sauce I always brought on our family camping trips, which was a favorite of theirs. We looked at old photograph albums and remembered happier times. Cleaning the house and weeding the garden suddenly became favorite occupations.

One night, Roger and I sat up talking. Roger was having a difficult time facing the emotional reality that Janet was dying. For the first time he began sharing his feelings about their situation. "I just broke apart when I found out," he said. "Every time I tried to talk about it, I started crying so hard I couldn't speak. I couldn't believe something like this could happen to us. I didn't want to talk about it, I just wanted it to go away. Mostly, I just didn't want to lose her."

"Our minister came to visit Janet a few weeks ago. Janet wanted to discuss arrangements for her funeral. She told our minister she isn't afraid to die, and I don't think she is, but I know she thought about dying a lot. One day, when she thought she was alone, I saw her look at her reflection in the bedroom mirror and slowly wave goodbye to her image. That nearly broke my heart."

Later that night, Roger shared the grief he had been holding inside for all those months with Janet. He was able to tell her he knew she had to leave him. He added that he was stronger now and although it would be difficult to let her go, he would be all right. It was a relief to hear him say that. I had the feeling Janet was waiting for Roger to get strong enough to cope with her dying before she was willing to let go of life.

The next morning the roses in Janet's garden started blooming. Knowing how much Janet loved her roses, Lucy and Jenny picked several and set them in a vase by her bedside. As the day progressed there was a noticeable change in Janet's breathing. The hospice nurse arrived and confirmed that it looked like Janet was nearing the end. We gathered around Janet's bed, holding her hands and saying our individual prayers. Roger was in tears as he struggled with his feelings of grief. Suddenly there was a knock at the door. We looked at one another, wondering who could be interrupting us at such a moment. Roger reluctantly rose and, wiping away his tears with the back of his hand, walked slowly to open the door.

On the step stood one of Roger's neighbors. The man looked a little confused and said apologetically, "I really don't know why I am standing here. I was driving by your house and I had a sudden urge to come see you." Roger explained that he couldn't invite the man in right now, he was busy. His wife was dying. The man apologized again for the interruption and said, "My wife died a year ago. At the time it hurt so much I thought I couldn't go on. But I got through it. I miss her terribly, of course, but somehow you do get through it. If there is anything, I can do for you, just let me know." With that, the man turned and left. Roger was perceptibly calmer when he returned to Janet's bedside. I don't know what angel was responsible for sending this neighbor, but I sent her a special prayer of gratitude.

As she neared the end, Janet momentarily regained consciousness. She opened her eyes and slowly looked into each of the faces gathered around her. Then her eyes closed, she gave one last sigh, and was gone. Suddenly, the room which had seemed so full a minute ago felt very empty. It was over. She was at peace.

The next day one of Janet's friends brought Roger a letter that Janet had written several months before. Janet had instructed her friend to give it to Roger after her death. The letter contained Janet's final messages for Roger and her children. It ended with the words, "I know I will die when the roses bloom. I will always love you and keep you close to my heart."

Several years after Janet's death, Roger met and married a wonderful woman. Although it seemed a little awkward at first, we became good friends. Janet's children are doing well, and her grandchildren are rapidly growing into wonderful young adults. We all get together whenever time allows. Being with Janet reminded me once again how precious life is and how quickly it can be taken away. I returned to my hospice work with a deeper appreciation for the process of dying and all its mysteries. I often think about a comment Mitch made just after his mother's death. "Mom's dying," he said to me, "was the most awful/awesome experience I have ever had." It was, indeed, Mitchell. It was indeed.

CHUCK AND DOT

There are so many different ways to say goodbye.

Caring for aging parents can be very rewarding but also brings its share of frustration, especially when a parent or parents refuse to listen to our very good advice. This is the story of the reward/frustration dynamic I experienced during the years I helped care for my own parents.

Dorothy and Charles, or Chuck and Dot, as my three brothers affectionately called them, lived most of their lives in Montana. My dad ran an insurance and title company in our small town in eastern Montana. My mom worked as a social worker and eventually became head of the county welfare department.

When my parents retired, they began escaping the cold Montana winters by coming to our home in Tucson and staying in the small guest cottage on our property. Each year they came a few weeks earlier and returned to Montana a few weeks later. It seemed no matter how late they stayed, they always got caught in a spring snowstorm on their drive home. When my father, after years of smoking, was diagnosed with emphysema, my parents decided to move closer to their children. Since they were familiar with Tucson from their years of wintering there, Tucson seemed the logical place to relocate. The fact that I was a nurse was a bonus.

My father had been reluctant to make a permanent move to Tucson because of the extreme summer temperatures. He often said, "You can always put more clothes on when it's cold, but there's not much you can do if it's hot." Once the move was completed, however, my father became a one-man Chamber of Commerce for the city of Tucson. During the winter, he loved to call friends still living in Montana. He would cheerily ask, "What's the temperature up there?" and then announce the Tucson temperature, which was usually 40 to 50 degrees warmer. In the summer when Montana friends would kid him about the heat, he was quick to point out that it was a dry heat, not like that humid heat in the Midwest. "Why with air conditioning, you hardly noticed it," he would claim.

Chuck and Dot quickly settled into their new lives. They found an attractive three-bedroom apartment several miles from our house. Mom and I had fun picking out furniture and decorating their new home. It wasn't long before my parents made friends with other retirees living in their apartment complex. The couple started playing bridge and hosting small dinner parties. My parents also entertained a constant stream of out-of-town visitors. Mom, who was a dynamo of energy, would arrange marathon sightseeing trips around the state, which left her visitors and my dad exhausted. We all wondered where she got her energy.

Sadly, as Dad grew older, he developed a fear of being cheated. He often quoted stories he had read concerning Medicare fraud or elders being bilked out of their savings by some "shyster". "Whenever a doctor ordered a test, procedure or a new medication for either parent, Dad would check with me to make sure what was ordered was "medically necessary" and not just some doctor running up "unnecessary medical bills to make a profit."

Strangers weren't the only targets of Dad's distrust. His offspring also came under suspicion. Dad was hesitant about adding any of his children's names to his checking or savings accounts. Logically Dad knew it was a good idea if one of his children could access funds in case of an emergency, but he could not quite bring himself to trust any of us enough to give us access to any of his money. Although no one questioned his decision, he justified his position by citing examples of stories he had heard where children had taken advantage of such arrangements and squandered their parents' savings.

Despite Dad's suspicious nature, we enjoyed having my parents living nearby. They dropped in frequently for dinner or to watch the local college football and basketball teams play on TV. We attended graduations and school events, celebrated holidays and birthdays together.

Several years after their relocation, I got a call one day from my father while I was at work. Dad sounded very upset. He had become concerned when my mother failed to get up at her usual time. When she still hadn't appeared for breakfast, Dad went to check on her and found her sound asleep. He called her name and when she didn't respond, he gently shook her. Mom opened her eyes but seemed very drowsy and fell right back to sleep. "Something's not right," Dad said. "I know something is wrong. What should I do?"

I instructed Dad to call the paramedics and have Mom taken to the hospital where I would meet them. When I arrived, Mom was in the Emergency Department being examined by her physician. The doctor explained he felt Mom had suffered a stroke. The plan was to admit her to the telemetry unit where she could be closely monitored.

Unfortunately, the doctor's diagnosis was correct. Mother's stroke left her with partial paralysis on the right side of her body. After intensive physical therapy and a great deal of hard work on Mom's part, she was able to learn to walk again using a cane. Sadly, she never regained the use of her right hand.

A month later Mom was discharged from the Rehab Center. Despite Mom's stroke, my parents insisted on remaining in their own apartment. My pleas for them to move into our guest cottage fell on deaf ears. Dad found himself an instant caregiver, a role he had never anticipated assuming. Unlike my brothers, who were accomplished cooks and cleaners, thanks to my mother's tutoring, my father, a typical male of his time, was not very self-sufficient. He had managed through the years to learn to fix himself breakfast and lunch. His standard fare included coffee, juice and cereal for breakfast, followed by tuna and crackers topped off with three or four Oreo cookies for lunch. He depended on Mom to fix his dinners, do the laundry, house cleaning and grocery shopping. Suddenly finding himself the manager of their household, he was completely lost.

My brothers arrived and took turns lending a hand until Dad learned how to handle his new caregiver role, teaching Dad the art of house-keeping. These lessons included everything from how to make out a grocery list (something Dad found totally bewildering at first) to how to do laundry. Although my parents could easily afford to hire help, my father who prided himself on his Scottish thriftiness, flatly refused to consider the suggestion.

Dad had no problem providing breakfasts and lunches for the two of them. Dinners proved more challenging. My parents tried Meals on Wheels, but after two weeks discontinued the service, claiming the food didn't taste good. Dad then announced he was perfectly capable of cooking their dinners himself. When I made inquiries as to how he was doing with his gastronomic adventures, Dad became suspiciously vague and uninformative. The mystery of how dinners were appearing on my parents' table was solved when one of my brothers, while visiting, dis-covered the menus for every takeout restaurant in a two-mile radius hanging on my parents' refrigerator. Even more telling was the fact that Dad had most of the menus memorized! Takeout meals or TV dinners became their standard fare, supplemented with weekly dinners at my house with plenty of leftovers to take home.

Watching my parents struggle with the change that had occurred in their lives was difficult. They wanted so badly to hang onto their inde-pendence despite their desperate need for help. Knowing this, it was with some trepidation that I suggested we tour some of the senior living situations that were so abundant in the Tucson area. As a community nurse, I had been in and out of most of these facilities while visiting pa-tients and was very familiar with what each had to offer. My parents reluctantly agreed to a tour. My dad insisted, however, that we limit the tour to only one facility, as he didn't want to spend the day, "traipsing all over Tucson". I carefully selected a senior complex I thought my par-ents would like, one which offered the services that best fit their needs. The following Saturday we arrived at the chosen facility. Since the tour involved a lot of walking, I pushed Mom in a wheelchair, while my father with his oxygen tank slung over his shoulder trudged along behind us. My parents viewed the well-appointed apartments, the various activity rooms, the dining room where we sampled a meal and the gardens and pool without comment. I couldn't tell how they were responding to the information our chatty guide was providing. I had my fingers crossed.

When we finished our visit, my parents made several polite comments about how nice the place was and said they would have to "give moving there some serious thought." On our way back to their apartment, I turned to my father and asked if he had noticed anything about the people living in the place we had visited. "Yeah," Dad laughed. "They were all in better shape than we are." I nodded, hoping the message was beginning to sink in and my parents would finally realize their need to move to a place where they could get the help they needed. I was especially concerned about my dad, who was steadily growing weaker, finding it increasingly difficult to carry out his caregiver duties.

Several days went by and I received no word from my parents. Curious to learn what they had decided, I stopped by their apartment. "We talked about that place you showed us, dear," my mother said with a smile, in answer to my question. "But I don't think we want to move out of our apartment just yet." When I asked why, she replied, "Those places are so small, we wouldn't have any room for your brothers to stay when they come to visit. So, I just don't think it's what we want to do."

"Mom, can't you see how badly you need help?" I groaned silently to myself. Disappointed with their decision, I quietly muttered to myself the mantra one of my co-workers had coined for just these situations. "Competent people have the legal right to make unwise decisions. Competent people have the legal right to make unwise decisions. Competent people ...." Well, you get the idea. I knew better than to argue with these two about their decision or to question the logic behind it. Instead, I tried a different tact. "Why don't you think about putting your name on the list for an apartment?" I suggested. "There's a long wait, especially for the two-bedroom apartment you want. It may be quite a while before one is available. You can always turn the apartment down if you aren't ready to make a move when your name comes up," I assured them. "Putting your name down now might give you more options later if you need them." My parents reluctantly agreed to have their names put on the waiting list. I knew it was more to appease me than to make plans for care they might need in the future.

In other ways my parents were very realistic about the tasks they needed to complete. Several months after our "grand facility tour," the family gathered to celebrate Thanksgiving. Our daughters who were away at college, had come home to celebrate the holiday with us, bringing along assorted friends and roommates. Family plus invited guests were seated around a table laden with the traditional Thanksgiving feast. My dad, as the family elder, said the blessing. Everyone began filling their plates, chatting to those seated nearby. During a lull in the conversation my mother, who had been very quiet, suddenly sat up very straight and announced in a loud clear voice, "Say, did you know I'm going to be cremated?" There was an audible gasp from those around the table, no one knowing quite what to say to my mother, who sat there beaming proudly. The first to recover was my youngest daughter, Nicole who was seated next to her grandmother. Nicole turned to her and said in her gentlest of voices, "That's wonderful, Granny! You sound very pleased about that. Sounds like you have everything all planned out." To this day during Thanksgiving dinner some family member will remark, "Say, did you know I'm going to be cremated?" and smiles break out around the table. For a moment Mom's loving presence can be felt among us.

******

My parents continued to live independently for several years after Mom's stroke. Because of his emphysema, my father had frequent bouts of pneumonia and was hospitalized several times in the ensuing years. Mom would come stay with us when this occurred. My father

13

would join her after he was discharged, staying with us until he regained his strength. As soon as Dad felt he had sufficiently recovered, the couple would insist on returning to their own apartment and their struggles would continue.

Because of his poor health, my father was convinced that he would be the first to die. He set about making plans for my mother's care after he was gone. He created a family trust and had an attorney draw up living wills and Medical and Financial Powers of Attorneys for the two of them. I was named their Medical Power of Attorney, giving me the right to make health care decisions for them if they were unable to do so for themselves. One of my brothers, Bill, and I were co-executors of the trust. The reasoning behind selecting the two of us was that my brother was very good at managing and investing money. I, on the other hand, would know what kind of care my mother needed. Dad felt we would make a good team and he was right.

I was at work one afternoon when my father called to report that my mother had fallen. She was unable to get up and he was too weak to help her, so he had called the paramedics. He said, "The paramedics are insisting that your mother should go to the hospital. I don't think that's really necessary, but I told them to talk to you about it."

I spoke to a paramedic, who informed me that Mom had a developed a very rapid heart rate, resulting in a drop in her blood pressure, which had probably caused her fall. She needed to be transported to the hospital for treatment. I agreed with their assessment and Dad reluctantly gave his consent. I called my husband asking him to meet me at the hospital.

My mother, after being examined in the Emergency Department by her cardiologist, was admitted to the hospital and moved to a private room. Once she was comfortably situated, my husband and I decided to dash home, feed our dog and cat and grab a quick dinner. As we were finishing our chores, we received a call from the hospital. Mom had lost consciousness for a few moments. She had quickly recovered, but as a precaution she was being moved to the Intensive Care Unit, where her condition could be more closely monitored. Mom seemed fine, the nurse reassured us, but she wanted to let us know Mom had been moved.

My husband drove as we dashed back to the hospital. Sitting beside him, worried about my mother, I had a very strange experience. I heard a voice in my mind say to me quite sternly, "You need to address your mother's code status. You need to get a do-not-resuscitate (DNR) order on her chart tonight. This is important. You need to listen. You need to do this." I was startled to say the least. My first reaction was to pretend I had heard nothing and to disregard what I was being told to do. I dreaded the idea of upsetting Dad further by talking to him about this. What would be the reaction of the nurses and doctors if I walked into the hospital and asked that such an order be put on Mom's chart? I would look foolish and demanding. I knew, however, I needed to pay attention to what I was being told to do, regardless of how foolish I might look or feel. Mom was very frail. If someone tried to do chest compression on her fragile ribs she would wind up with multiple, painful fractures. I had no choice, I needed to do what I had been asked to do.

When we arrived at the hospital, I found Mom sitting up in bed eating dinner and chatting with the nurses. Although Mom seemed to be doing well, her nurse was concerned. "She looks fine but some of her blood gases aren't as good as I'd like," her nurse reported. "I can't put my finger on anything specific, but I feel like something's going on."

The nurse's comment reinforced my determination. I gathered up my courage and approached Dad, who was too distraught to really understand what I was asking. "Do whatever you think is best, honey," was his response to my request. When I spoke to the nurse about getting a DNR order she looked relieved, and said, "I think that is a very good idea." She promptly contacted the doctor and handed me the phone. Dr. Holloway was a dear, compassionate man who had been treating my parents for several years. When I asked him to write the DNR order, I could tell he was taken aback by my unexpected request. "I really don't

15

think an order like that is necessary," Dr. Holloway said, sounding puzzled. "Your mom just had a little reaction to one of the medications she was given. I'm sure she'll be fine. I'll probably discharge her in a couple of days."

"I know her condition doesn't appear serious," I agreed, "but I would really rest easier if we have a DNR order on her chart just in case."

"All right," the doctor reluctantly agreed." But just so you know, I plan to treat whatever is wrong with her aggressively." I agreed that this was what the family wanted also. "But in the event that she stops breathing and her heart stops beating, we don't want her resuscitated," I reiterated.

"Okay, if it makes you feel better, I will have one of the nurses write the order," the doctor finally agreed. After the order was written Mom's nurse gave me a hug and said, "You're a good daughter."

Mom was brushing her teeth and asking for another blanket when I kissed her goodbye. She gave me a list of things she wanted brought to the hospital the next morning and cheerily waved us on our way. We walked out the door without a backward glance.

We dropped Dad off at their apartment and hurried on home. The phone was ringing when my husband and I walked into the house. It was the hospital. My mom had died quite suddenly just after we left. Without warning, her heart had simply stopped beating. Her death had come quietly and peacefully. "Aw, Mom," I thought when I heard the news, "I wish I had been with you. I should have stayed."

We returned to the hospital after picking up Dad. Knowing Mom planned to be cremated, we wanted to say a final goodbye. Mom's nurse was waiting for us when we arrived. "Dr. Holloway left a message for you to call him as soon as you got here," she said. When the doctor came to the phone his first words were, "I don't know what to tell you. I never expected this. I am so sorry. I know this must be an awful shock. How is your dad doing?"

Dad and I went to see Dr. Holloway several weeks later to discuss Mom's death. I asked the doctor if he had any idea what had happened. The doctor had read through Mom's chart looking for clues. From what was written, he concluded that my mother had had another massive stroke, one so devastating that it had caused her heart to suddenly stop functioning.

I was so grateful for the message instructing me to obtain the DNR order. Without it, the nurses by law would have been forced to try to resuscitate Mom. Doing chest compression would have probably broken her ribs, causing Mom a great deal of unnecessary pain. Once revived, she would have been put on a respirator, which would have forced her to breathe. The thought of Mom in pain and on a respirator while the family sat around deciding when to take her off life support was horrible. It was hard enough to lose my Mom. Thank goodness we were spared the experience of watching her go through unnecessary pain and suffering.

My dad had always been someone who never displayed feelings, someone who prided himself on approaching any situation rationally and logically. When one of his teenagers was late coming home, my mother would pace the floor worrying that something had happened, visualizing her child lying injured or dead in a ditch somewhere after a car accident. My father, on the other hand, would go off to bed stating there was no use staying up as there was nothing he could do about the situation. If something bad had actually happened, Dad believed he would be better able to cope with a tragedy if he had gotten a good night's sleep. My three brothers (always quick to hand out nicknames) promptly labeled Dad "Mr. Spock" and teased him about his lack of emotional response.

With my mother's death, Dad seemed to melt emotionally, like the sudden thawing of an iceberg. He was devastated by his wife's unexpected death. Not only had he lost his partner of over fifty years, he had lost his purpose in life as well, his job as caregiver. Dad became very depressed, overwhelmed by a grief he had no language to express. All Dad was able to say was "I hurt. I have a pain in my chest." When I first heard him say this, I was concerned my father might be having a heart attack. When I questioned him further about this pain, his response was always the same, "I hurt, I hurt because of your mother." He stopped eating and slept very little, staying up late at night watching TV. His life felt hopeless.

Dad's physician started him on an antidepressant. Knowing these medications take several weeks to work, I was concerned that my father, in his fragile state, could not survive that long without severe physical consequences. I considered bringing him to live with us, but since my husband and I both worked, Dad would be alone all day, so this did not appear to be a good solution. One of the local hospitals offered an inpatient treatment program designed especially for seniors with depression. When I mentioned this program to Dad, he readily agreed to be admitted. Knowing how much my father distrusted the medical system, I realized just how desperate he had become. I contacted his doctor and arrangements were made for Dad's admission. During his hospitalization my father's depression quickly improved with the combination of antidepressant medications and group therapy. Two weeks later my father was discharged.

I was determined not to let Dad return to his apartment, where I feared he would once again be overwhelmed by depression. I contacted the retirement complex my parents had toured. The director said she had been trying to contact my parents to let them know their name had come to the top of the waiting list and a two-bedroom apartment had just become available. A miracle! Even more miraculous, my father agreed to move in.

My father settled into his new apartment and instantly experienced a wave of popularity sparked by the fact that the number of women living in the facility greatly outnumbered the men. Dad, who was still a good-looking man at eighty-four, tall, tanned, with a full head of glossy white hair, was an instant hit with the ladies. They vied for his attention and flooded Dad with invitations. Embarrassed by all the fuss being made over him, my father was at a loss as to how to handle the situation. He was rescued when a woman named Phyllis moved in next door. The two of them became close friends, much to the disappointment of numerous female residents. Phyllis and Dad went everywhere together. At Dad's request, Phyllis was included in all our family dinners and holiday celebrations. Slowly, Dad began to enjoy life again.

Emotionally, Mom's death created a permanent change in Dad. As his depression dissipated Dad became much more open and loving. He began calling me Pumpkin, a nickname he had used when I was a little girl. He told me how much I was loved and how much he appreciated everything my husband Vic and I had done for him. When he put my name on his checking account so I could access his money in an emergency, I knew the change was deep and far-reaching.

Several years later, Dad's emphysema entered its final stage. My father was dying. I contacted hospice and we moved Dad from his apartment to our home where I could care for him. Dad expressed the wish to see his children and grandchildren one last time. The family was contacted and a travel plan for each family member was devised. Originally, family members were scheduled to visit Dad in small numbers, a few people at a time. These visits were to be extended over several weeks so Dad would not be overwhelmed by large numbers of people. When it became obvious that my father's condition was deteriorating more rapidly than expected, the entire family hastily made plans to travel to Tucson.

Caring for my father plus providing for all the visitors required organization. A family meeting was held where people divided up the day-to-day chores. My niece Marie and her partner Kitty, an amateur chef, volunteered to take over making dinner. My brothers became errand runners and chauffeurs and helped out wherever needed. The sisters-in-laws took over laundry and house cleaning. My daughter Nicole, who is also a nurse, helped me with Dad's care while her husband assumed full-time responsibility for their two-year-old son. Hospice was there to adjust my father's medication, provide emotional support and help with his personal care. People took turns sitting by Dad's bedside, taking this opportunity to say their goodbyes. The gathering became a strange sort of family reunion. We exchanged childhood remembrances and supported one another through the stress of losing our father. Several days later, Dad quietly slipped into a coma. He died peacefully, surrounded by the people who loved him.

Hospice was notified, and a nurse came out and pronounced Dad legally dead. We asked her to delay calling the mortuary, while the family gathered to say their final goodbyes.

Several days before Dad's death, our family decided we wanted to have our own private ceremony when Dad died. My youngest brother Ted had taken on the task of planning this service. Shortly after my father's death, the family gathered in his room. We stood in a circle surrounding my dad. A large candle representing my father was lit and set on a table by his bedside, and several of Dad's favorite hymns were sung. Then one by one each family member took a smaller candle from a nearby pile, lit it from the larger candle and talked about what having Dad in their lives had meant to them. We closed our ceremony by saying several prayers and singing "Now the Day is Over," our faces lit by the candles we were holding, our eyes bright with unshed tears. It was a comforting way to say our goodbyes to someone whose life had touched us all.

A funeral was held several days later at the local Episcopal church which my parents had attended. Saddened as we were by my father's death, we also felt a sense of satisfaction. We had done it. We had been able to give Dad his final wish, to die at home in a room overlooking his beloved Catalina Mountains, surrounded by the people he loved.

During his last few years of life, Dad completed a tremendous emotional journey. He transformed from Mr. Spock, an emotionally unavailable, logical, distrusting person, into a warm, loving caring, trusting father. It was truly remarkable to watch this change take place and to finally experience the warm loving relationship I had always wanted with him. At times, I still feel his calm, loving presence.

RALPH JONES

How much control do we actually have over when our final moment occurs?

Whenever I speak with community groups about hospice, I find people want information about the physical, emotional and spiritual changes that one goes through during the process of dying. Among the many questions asked is, "How much do we control when our death will occur?" Often individuals who asked this question had experienced a family member who seemed to hang on until a loved one arrived, a baby was born, or a wedding took place, then dying hours after the event had occurred. I often answered these types of questions by talking about my experience with Mr. Jones.

Ralph Jones was admitted to our hospice program after being diagnosed with stage four lung cancer with widespread metastases. His physician, Dr. Logan, felt the disease had progressed too far for treatment to be effective. Mr. Jones, who did not want to go through the side effects of either chemotherapy or radiation, readily agreed with his physician's recommendation of not treating his cancer. Several of Mr. Jones' adult children, who were present during this appointment, became angry when learning that Mr. Jones was seriously ill, yet refusing treatment. His children felt their father was just giving up. A heated discussion followed, with the family insisting on treatment and Mr. Jones, with the backing of his physician, refusing. Finally, Dr. Logan told the family the decision had been made and their father was being referred to hospice. Still upset, the family stormed out of the physician's office, vowing to get a second opinion.

Later that afternoon when Dr. Logan spoke to the hospice intake nurse, he described the angry scene that had taken place in his office. He wanted the hospice staff to be aware of the dynamics occurring within the family.

I was the home care nurse assigned to work with the Jones. Knowing I was about to face a potentially volatile situation, I took a deep breath as I stood on their doorstep and centered myself before ringing the bell.

The doorbell was answered by May, Mr. Jones's youngest daughter. May ushered me into the living room, where I introduced myself to Mr. Jones, who stood with some difficulty, shook my hand and requested I just call him Ralph.

Before I had a chance to introduce myself to his two other children, Richard and Daisy, they began to pepper me with questions: Why wasn't their dad being treated? Doesn't a doctor have to treat someone if they were sick? Did I think it was alright for their dad to just give up?

Ralph held up his hand, saying, "Quit bothering the nurse. This lady has come to do a job; let her do it." With this, the family settled down. I told them I could see how concerned they were about their father and that I would sit down and talk with them after I finished examining their dad and getting his medical history.

Ralph was a tall somewhat gruff, eighty-five-year-old who had worked as an electrician until he retired in his early seventies. He had been married for sixty-three years to his high school sweetheart Emily. Their youngest daughter May lived with the couple. May, who was in her forties, had a poorly controlled seizure disorder which prevented her from driving or holding a steady job. Although unable to work outside the home, May was able to help her mother with the gardening and household chores. The couple's two older children, Richard and Daisy, were both married and lived nearby.

After completing Ralph's examination, I sat down with his children, listened to their concerns and answered their questions regarding their father's condition. Throughout our discussion, the children kept insisting that somehow, despite what the doctor and I told them, their dad would "beat this thing." At the end of the visit I left the house realizing nothing was going to convince the family that their father was dying. Their goal had become to rally around their dad and help him defeat his cancer.

As I continued to visit Ralph, I began to understand why Ralph was so important to his family. Ralph was the family patriarch. He made all the important decisions, not only for himself and Emily but for the entire family. Where his children lived, who they married, and what jobs they accepted had all been decided by him. The family was so reliant on his guidance, they literally were unable to make decisions for themselves.

Although the older children were in their late forties, emotionally they had never left their parents' home and had no real lives of their own. Each weekday evening, both married children together with their families, arrived after work for dinner with their parents. Every weekend found the entire family either gathered in the Jones's living room watching TV or sitting in their parents' small backyard talking. During these family gatherings, arguments frequently broke out as the siblings vied for Ralph's attention and approval. When these quarrels occurred, Ralph stepped in quickly to stop the dispute before the disagreement could escalate.

For the first few months after Ralph's admission to hospice, life in the Jones household went on as usual. Ralph was eating well and taking regular walks around the block. Despite regular visits from the hospice team, the family continued to deny the fact that Ralph was terminally ill. Much to his frustration, whenever Ralph attempted to discuss his illness with them, or to make plans for after he was gone, the family refused to talk about his dying and quickly changed the subject. They seemed to have an "if we don't admit he is dying, then it won't happen," attitude. I made no attempt to confront the family's denial, recognizing that sometimes individuals need time in order to develop the inner strength to face a painful situation. As time passed, I knew it would become obvious to all that Ralph was dying.

During the next several months, changes in Ralph's condition became increasingly apparent, as a slightly overweight, forceful man became a frail and fragile one. Ralph, who was always a big eater, now barely touch his food despite his family's pleas to eat more to "keep up your strength." As his disease progressed, Ralph lost his booming voice and it became an effort for him to talk. It now took two people to get him out of bed or his favorite recliner. He needed continuous oxygen and became short of breath with the slightest exertion. He was too weak to walk to the mailbox, pay the bills or play with his grandchildren. A home-health aide came in three times a week to help him shower and shave.

The family found it difficult to see the strong husband and father they had always relied on now sick and needing help. Ralph also found it difficult to accept his growing weakness. He fought hard to maintain his independence, but eventually his condition left him no choice but to accept his family's assistance. My visits now included a new focus, teaching the family how to care for Ralph.

Although physically weak, Ralph retained his control over his family. He issued detailed instructions regarding tasks he wanted done and exactly how to do them. No one's performance measured up to Ralph's exacting specifications, and as his disease progressed, he became increasingly short-tempered and critical of his family's efforts to care for him. Ralph appeared determined to retain his role as family arbitrator and decision maker for as long as possible.

About six months after Ralph entered the hospice program, the on-call nurse received a frantic 2a.m. phone call from May. Ralph was struggling to breathe, and the family was frightened. When the nurse arrived at the Jones's home, she found Ralph exhausted and gasping for breath. Ralph was entering the final stage of his illness. Aware that his family would need intense emotional support through this final stage, the nurse suggested Ralph be admitted to the hospice's inpatient unit. After a brief discussion, Ralph agreed to the move. His family seemed relieved to hand over the responsibility of Ralph's care to "professionals."

Hospice inpatient units, unlike a regular hospital ward, are designed with patients' and families' needs in mind. There is a room equipped with comfortable chairs and couches where family and friends can gather. Snacks are kept in the refrigerator and a microwave oven is available for people who wish to bring in food. Visitors are welcome 24 hours a day and pets and children are encouraged to visit.

Once Ralph was admitted, his family arranged for at least one member to remain in his room 24 hours a day. They took turns sitting at his bedside, watching Ralph anxiously, looking for changes in his condition. Whenever Ralph's breathing slowed and he drifted off to sleep, a family member would shake him awake, crying, "Don't leave us, Daddy. Don't leave us." The family was determined not to let Ralph die. After several days of this, both Ralph and his family were exhausted.

One morning, I stopped by to see how Ralph and his family were doing. Ralph was awake when I arrived, and his face lit up when he saw me. I asked how he was feeling, and Ralph said the nurses were keeping him comfortable with "that magic elixir of theirs that helps my breathing." When I asked if there was something I could do for him, Ralph nodded his head "yes" and motioned me to come closer. I stepped toward the bed. He motioned again for me to move even closer. At his insistence, I kept moving until I was bent over him with my ear next to his mouth. He gestured toward his family and said in a soft whisper, "Can you get them out of here?" Startled, I looked at him questioningly. "Can you get them out of here so I can die?" He was looking straight at me, his eyes pleading. This man, who never asked help from anyone, looked desperate. "I'll see what I can do," I said, squeezing his shoulder.

I left his room and walked down the hall looking for our social worker. Finding her at the nurses' station, I asked if she had time to meet with the Jones family and help them make funeral arrangements, something the family had put off doing. When I reported to Ralph that the social worker wanted to see the family, he insisted they go meet with her, all the family, no exceptions.

The family reluctantly left the room, making me promise I would stay with Ralph until they returned.

As soon as the family disappeared, Ralph closed his eyes, took several deep breaths and began to relax. A few moments passed as Ralph's body became limp, appearing to melt right into the mattress. His breathing slowed, then stopped completely. An expression of peace settled over him. Ralph was gone. "Wow," I thought." "I can't believe he did it. That was amazing." I sat for several moments absorbing what I had just experienced, letting the reality of what had just happened settle in. As the impact of Ralph's passing subsided, I said a silent good-bye to him before walking down the hall to let his family know Ralph had died. I knew they was going to be very upset by Ralph's passing.

His family was still gathered around the table in the Family Room talking with the social worker when I walked in. As soon as they saw me, they guessed what had happened. Ralph was dead. Furious and feeling betrayed, the family began to question me angrily. "What happened?" "How could you let him die?" "Why didn't you stop him?" "Wasn't there anything you could do to bring him back?" "How could you let him go without us being there?" The family's grief and anger were palpable.

The chaplain, hearing the family's distress, came to help me comfort them. The two of us sat there listening as the family expressed their rage; first at their father for dying and then at me for letting it happen. Finally, as the intensity of their emotions faded, I spoke with the family acknowledging how much they loved Ralph and how hard it was going to be for them to go on without him. I explained that I felt Ralph had held onto life for as long as he could, knowing how much they loved and needed him. When Ralph reached the point where his body was no longer able to function, I explained, he had no choice but to go. Knowing the family was very religious, I added, "You were in a tug-of-war with God. He was calling Ralph home and you were holding on to Ralph, wanting to keep him with you. God won. He always does."

At first my words were greeted with silence, then several family members nodded in agreement as they began to understand what I was saying. Somewhat comforted, the family slowly left the room.

As the Joneses walked back to Ralph's room to say their goodbyes, I heard Ralph's son Richard say, "As soon as we leave here a couple of us need to go to the funeral home and finish the arrangements." I had an idea who was going to replace Ralph as family patriarch.

Afterthoughts

Experiences like the one I had with Ralph and his family make me suspect people, at least in some situations, have some control over when the moment of their death will occur and who is with them when their death takes place.

Survivors I've talked to frequently talk about how guilty they feel because a loved one died without the family member being physically present. As one widow stated, "I feel so awful every time I think about my husband's death. I stayed with Barney every minute toward the end because I knew he could go at any time. We had had such a good life together. We shared everything, so I couldn't imagine letting him die without me there holding his hand. I left for just a few minutes to go to the bathroom, and when I got back, he was gone. I hate the idea that I let him down. I let him die alone."

This widow's story is not unusual. Having a loved one die moments after family has left the room is a fairly common occurrence. I believe there are several reasons why this phenomenon occurs. When a strong bond exists between people, it is just too difficult for the dying person to let go and leave when someone they love is sitting next to them. Like Barney, the dying person often waits until his or her loved ones are no longer present before being able to take that final step of physical separation.

Dying individuals seem to develop an awareness of which family members have the emotional strength to be present when the death occurs. I feel Janet, for example, was very aware that her two daughters were emotionally overwhelmed by her dying. I was not surprised when her death occurred with only her son Mitch, her husband and myself present.

The personality of the dying person may also play a part in whether they choose to die alone. In my experience, very private persons who have been reluctant to share their thoughts and feelings with others also seem reluctant to share their death, often slipping away quietly and alone.

Certainly, many people die surrounded by family and friends and are comforted by their presence. Sometimes individuals seem to delay dying until a love one can get there. One woman I knew clung to life for a week until her son, who was in the army and station overseas, could get home to her. She died several hours after his arrival.

For most of us, much of the dying process remains a mystery. But there does appear to be some evidence that the dying individual not only has some control over when they die but also over who is with them when their death occurs

HELPING CHILDREN UNDERSTAND DEATH

The age of a child influences how he or she experiences the loss of a loved one.

Much has been written about how our society attempts to hide from facing the finality of death. Euphemisms such as "He is gone," "He has passed," "He's no longer with us," "He went to sleep," "Jesus took him," are examples of ways we soften the impact of our loss and protect ourselves from the emotional shock of losing someone we care about. When the death involves someone close to a child, these feelings of wanting to protect are intensified.

Each of us teaches our children about death according to our own individual customs and beliefs. A death of a pet is often the first death a child will experience. This was certainly what happened in our family.

My husband and I decided to surprise our daughter Ann with a beautiful long-haired gray kitten for her seventh birthday. She was thrilled and promptly named the kitten Missy. Ann spent hours playing with Missy and even managed to teach her to retrieve, a first in my experience with felines. One morning, several years after Missy's arrival, we found her lying on the patio limp and barely responsive. Ann sat in the back seat of the car cradling the sick cat in her lap while we drove to the vet. Our vet took one look at Missy and shook her head. She said the cat had somehow gotten into poison put out by the city to kill the large roof rats that had suddenly infested the area. Although the poison was placed high in trees and wires, sometimes it was blown down. The vet had seen several cats displaying the same symptoms in the past several days. There was nothing she could do to save Missy.

The doctor suggested we put Missy to sleep to spare her further suffering. Sadly, we agreed. Ann begged to stay with Missy and we reluctantly said yes, not sure if this was something Ann should be witnessing. Ann held her cat as the medication was injected, crying silently throughout the procedure. When it was over, Ann wrapped Missy in a towel the vet gave us and brought her home.

My daughter was devastated. I sat beside her feeling helpless, desperately trying to think of ways to console her. As Ann lay on her bed sobbing, I gently stroked her hair and began talking about how much I was also going to miss Missy and the things I had loved about her. Soon we were both crying. After what seemed like hours, Ann's sobs finally stopped. As she sat there drying her eyes, I asked if she would like to have a funeral for Missy. She tearfully nodded and we began to make our plans.

I found a sturdy shoe box which we decided would make a good casket. Ann carefully lined the box with an old flannel baby blanket she had been using for her dolls. She and her sister Nicole decorated the box with drawings of Missy's favorite things: mice, a ball, and a saucer of milk. When the "casket" was finished to my daughter's satisfaction, Ann gently placed Missy in it along with several of the cat's favorite toys. My husband helped Ann seal the lid with tape.

While the girls were making Missy's casket, their father dug a grave in a corner of the backyard. When everything was ready Ann solemnly placed the box in the freshly dug grave. Our family stood in a circle around the grave and at Ann's direction, we took turns recalling our favorite memory of Missy and sharing what we loved most about her. After the service, Ann and her dad finished burying the pet. Later, my husband helped the girls build a wooden marker for Missy's grave.

Bedtime that night was hard for Ann. She was accustomed to falling asleep cuddling her cat. The girls and I sat snuggled in Ann's bed while I read them a special book describing a heaven for pets. Afterward, I stayed with Ann until she fell asleep.

This became our family's "Death of a Pet" ritual, a ritual which was repeated several times throughout the years my girls were growing up. Through this ritual, my daughters began learning about the permanence of death and the many ways there are to express their grief.

Children, especially younger children, learn by asking questions. When I think about questioning children, my granddaughter Tamara immediately comes to mind. Tamara is the champion "asker" of questions in our family. When Tamara was four, my husband and I stayed with her while her parents went on vacation. Each day as my husband drove her to nursery school, she came up with what my husband came to call the "Question of the Day." These ranged from, "Why is the sky blue, Grandpa?" to "Why can't we drive on the sidewalk when the roads are full of cars and the sidewalk is empty?"

Tamara's questions were her way of trying to understand her world and what was happening in it. Often a child's first response when a death occurs is to begin asking questions. "What does it mean to die?" "Does it hurt?" "Will I die?" "Will you?" "What happens to our bodies?" While these questions are a child's attempt to make sense of what is happening, to a grieving adult their bluntness may feel startling.

When someone close to a child dies, it is important the child be told of the death by someone she knows and trusts. Be honest and let her know exactly what has happened. If the child asks questions, give her as much information as she seems to want. When she asks, "Why did Grandpa die?" a simple, "His heart just wore out" may be all the information the child wishes. Children will ask if they want to know more. In my experience, most children have a very real awareness of what they can and cannot handle emotionally.

This fact was really brought home to me one summer when I took my grandchildren and several of their friends to San Francisco for the day. The top attraction on my grandchildren's list of things they wanted to see was the Wax Museum at Fisherman's Wharf. Upon reaching the museum, we slowly wandered among the wax figures, the kids stopping to read about and carefully examine each exhibit. Much to my surprise, it was the historical figures that caused the most excitement. The children loved seeing legendary figures like Benjamin Franklin and Abraham Lincoln up-close and "in person."

As we walked along, the corridor took a sudden turn and we found ourselves in front of an archway decorated with skulls and grotesque figures. We had arrived at the entrance to the Chamber of Horrors. A sudden hush fell as the kids came to an abrupt halt. After a slight hesitation, the older children let out shouts of excitement and hurried off to see the Chamber's gruesome contents, my granddaughter Tamara leading the charge. Not everyone was eager to enter the chamber, however. Gregory, my six-year-old grandson was standing frozen in front of the archway, staring wide-eyed at the gruesome faces. Noticing Gregory's expression, I said, "There are some pretty scary things in this next part, Gregory. We don't have to go through there if you don't want to. We can use that passage over there and go around the scary stuff if you want."

"What sort of scary stuff, Grandma?" Gregory asked in a timid little voice. "Scenes of people being killed or tortured with lots of fake blood," I said. "We don't have to go through there; it's okay to go around," I assured him. "We'll do whatever you want to do."

Gregory thought for a long moment and then, wanting to be brave like the older kids, said, "I think I can do it, Grandma, but I might have to hold your hand." Gregory made it through the Chamber of Horrors without a problem, although halfway through I felt a small hand slip into mine.

Tamara greets new situations head-on and loves a challenge. I will always cherish a mental picture I have of nine-year-old Tamara on that same San Francisco trip, hanging tightly to the outside of a cable car as it goes down a steep San Francisco hill, a grimace on her face, eyes clenched shut. Afterwards, she admitted to feeling scared during the ride but added, "I just wanted to see if I could do it." Gregory is the exact opposite. He likes to stop and size up a new situation before jumping into it and he refuses to participate in anything he doesn't feel comfortable doing.

Whether a child feels cautious or courageous often depends on the situation they are facing. Gregory and Tamara both knew instinctively how they would respond to the situations facing them and what they could emotionally handle. The same is true when children are facing the death of someone they love. They know what they can handle emotionally when a family member dies. Too often families make decisions for their children rather than consulting them. For example, if a child is six or over, I recommend you ask the child whether he/she wants to attend the funeral. The child will know if he/she is emotionally equipped to handle the experience. Often attending some sort of memorial service makes younger members feel a part of the family and helps them move through their own grieving process.

The way death is viewed by a child varies according to his/her age. Children five and under have a difficult time realizing death is permanent and typically view death as a temporary condition, expecting the person who has died to come back to life and the child's world to return to normal. It's not unusual for children of this age to ask, "When is Grandpa coming over?" days or weeks after attending Grandpa's funeral. Often their belief in the impermanence of physical death is reinforced by stories, cartoons and video games.

Older children understand death is permanent. By about age seven many have experienced losing pets and understand what dying means. Although children in this age group feel sadness when someone they love dies, they also have a great curiosity about death.

My daughters' first experience of losing a family member occurred when my eighty-five-year-old grandmother Edna died unexpectedly. Edna was a remarkable woman, one I greatly admired. As a young woman she had come to Montana with her family and had "proved-up" her own homestead, living summers in a sod house on her 320 acres of prairie. During the winters, she returned home to Indiana where she taught school. Eventually she married and made Montana her home. As kids, we loved visiting our grandmother. In addition to reading us stories, she taught us how to play games like I Spy and Cat's Cradle. We spent summer days pulling weeds with her in the vegetable garden and winter evenings husking home-grown popcorn and pulling taffy.

When she reached her eighties, Edna began experiencing small strokes or TIAs. At first, these episodes did not seem to affect her. Over time, however, my grandmother suffered memory loss, which affected her ability to care for herself. Eventually she was moved to a nearby home which provided assisted care. My grandfather remained in their house, visiting Edna daily.

Because of her mental impairment, and because we lived miles away in California, my children (Edna's great-grandchildren) never had a close relationship with her. The last time I took the girls to see her, Edna no longer recognized me and was unable to interact with her great-grand-daughters.

Although Edna had been steadily declining over the years, her death, when it occurred, felt sudden. As soon as we received the news of Edna's passing, we began making travel arrangements. When we arrived at my parent's home, we were surrounded by grieving relatives. Ann, now nine, Nicole five, and their cousin Marie, who was seven, did not know how to behave among people who were obviously very upset. Sensing their uneasiness, I suggested the girls come with me to the funeral home to say a private goodbye to Edna. They eagerly agreed.

As I started backing the car out of my parents' driveway the cousins began peppering me with questions, they hadn't felt comfortable asking in front of family. "Will we see her body?" "Will she be in a casket?" "How do they know she's really dead; what if she's only sleeping?" Their questions seemed endless and I struggled to find answers.

When we arrived, the girls, looking very serious and a little scared, entered the mortuary. The viewing room was empty except for a few chairs and Edna's casket. Approaching the casket, each girl took a cautious peak inside. Relief flooded across their faces as they saw what appeared to be their great-grandmother peacefully sleeping. "She looks beautiful," Ann whispered. "She doesn't look dead at all."

"Can I touch her?" asked Marie, the most adventurous of the three. "Go ahead," I said. "Touch her hand or cheek if you like." "She's so cold. It doesn't feel like skin at all." "Why is that?" Marie asked. Before I could respond, Nicole piped up, "Do they really drain the blood out? Is that what makes her so cold?"

Just then the viewing room door opened and the funeral home director, Mr. Bolton, walked in. Mr. Bolton had known me since I was a child. He had heard I was at the mortuary with Edna's great-granddaughters and had stopped by to express his condolences and to see how we were doing. I explained to Mr. Bolton that the girls had questions about how bodies were prepared for burial and asked if he would be willing to talk to them. Looking surprised, he agreed to my request.

The trio were delighted and began peppering him with questions. "Why do you take the blood out?" "How do you drain it?" "How do you know for sure someone's dead?" As Mr. Bolton began answering the girls' questions. he got caught up in their enthusiasm and in his role of instructor. "Would you like to see the room where we prepare the bodies?" he asked, giving me a quick questioning "Is this all right with you?" look. I nodded my consent. The girls were ecstatic and could barely contain their excitement as we trooped off to the embalming room. I tried not to think about how this experience would appear as the star feature in those "How I Spent My Summer" essays kids write when they return to school and what their teachers would think of my parenting.

Mr. Bolton was wonderful with the girls. He answered each of their questions very seriously. He explained in great detail how embalming was done, showing them the drain through which the body fluids were flushed during the procedure. He let them look at makeup kits and fillers used to help even sick great-grandmothers look as though they are peacefully sleeping. He allowed the girls to feel the inside of caskets and showed them where hair was washed and styled. and the bodies were dressed. The girls were particularly impressed when shown the materials used to disguise wounds. Mr. Bolton answered questions about how you know when someone is really dead and not just sleeping. He confirmed that no hair and fingernails do not continue to grow for a while after someone dies. He was patient and calm, portraying no signs of shock at the bluntness of their questions. Lord only knows what he was thinking. Finally, the flood of questions came to an end. The trio's heartfelt thank yous to Mr. Bolton had a sincerity about them that I had seldom heard from those three mischievous young girls.

We returned to the visitation room to say a last goodbye. The girls sat quietly, as I shared some of my favorite memories of time spent with Edna and how important she was to me. As we were leaving, the cousins decided they would like to do something special for their great-grandmother, something from just the three of them. We made a stop at the local florist who had exactly what the girls wanted, a simple arrangement of yellow roses, Edna's favorite flower, which would be placed next to her casket.

The funeral the next day was very emotional for all of us. Various family members shared their favorite memories of Edna. The girls sat quietly through the service laughing at some of the funny stories that were told and joining in the hymns and prayers. I saw Ann become teary when her great-grandfather Daniel passed Edna's casket and said, "I'll be joining you soon, Honey," to his wife of sixty-four years. Daniel kept his promise. He died in his sleep a year later.

Afterthoughts

When someone a child feels emotionally close to dies, the child may feel intense grief. Because most children have less life experience than an adult, they often need help finding ways to identify and express their emotions. One way to help them is by sharing your own. Talk to the child about your own feelings of sadness and loss, let children see your tears. Discuss with them things you miss about the person who has died, and what is hard for you to do alone. Sharing your grief in a way that doesn't overwhelm, gives a child permission to feel his/her own.

Whether attending the funeral, drawing a goodbye picture, writing a letter to the deceased or picking out flowers, it is important that children have an opportunity to participate in the ritual of saying goodbye. If a child decides to attend the funeral or memorial service, prepare her for the experience. Explain that a funeral is a special time for people who loved the deceased to say their goodbyes together. Discuss the service so the child knows what to expect. If there is an open casket, let the child decide whether to approach the casket to say goodbye. When younger children are attending a funeral, have someone available to-ztake youngsters out and stay with them if the children feel uncomfortable with the experience. When prepared, many children find attending the funeral comforting and receive a sense of closure from the experience.

It is not uncommon to seemingly recover from a death only to find the grief reoccurs, especially during holidays, on birthdays or other special occasions. Whenever my grandchildren do something particularly touching or funny, I find myself wishing my mom was there to enjoy the moment with me. She would have loved it. For an instant my grief comes rushing back and I am overwhelmed with sadness. In this sense, grief is never completely gone but can return to catch us and our children by surprise. As adults, we need to watch for those moments when our children are struggling and help them name and express what they are feeling.

Grief is triggered by many different life events: moving, changing jobs, a new school, children leaving home, a friend moving away, divorce, as well the more obvious death of a loved one. When we teach our children how to recognize when they are grieving and show them ways to express their sadness, we are giving them emotional tools which will help them cope not only with the death of a loved one but with other losses they will experience throughout their lives

GALINA

Somewhere underneath the changes caused by Alzheimer's, the real person remains intact.

One of the most painful experiences for a family is watching someone they love develop Alzheimer's Disease. Our family shared this experience when my mother-in-law Galina was diagnosed with the disease.

Galina was born in Russia. Two years following the arrest and execution of her husband during the 1937 purge of Ukraine, Galina, together with her three-year-old son Victor, fled across the Russian border into Poland. Several months later, Poland was invaded by Germany and mother and son found themselves in the center of World War Two. Somehow the two managed to survive. Three years after the war ended, Galina and her now 13-year-old son immigrated to the United States, settling in Palo Alto, California.

The next few years were spent adjusting to life in their new country. The two rented a small house and Vic started high school and eventually graduated from college. Galina found work making salads in the kitchen of a nearby college. Shortly after I moved to California in 1960, a mutual friend introduced Vic and me and the two of us were married two years later.

Galina had very mixed feelings about our marriage. She wanted Vic to be happy and realized the importance of his having a family of his own; but the actual experience of having him move out of the house they had shared for the last twelve years was another thing altogether. Because the two had survived a horrendous ordeal together, they had forged an unusually close relationship. Galina had never lived alone and depended on Vic to take her to and from work, pay the monthly bills and pick her up every Saturday after she had finished the weekly grocery shopping. Adjusting to her son's marriage and learning to be independent wasn't going to be easy.

My relationship with Galina was a rocky one from the start. Because of her Russian upbringing, Galina expected a quiet, obedient and respectful daughter-in-law, one who asked for and followed her mother-in-law's advice. Galina also wanted the three of us to eat dinner together every night and she assumed Vic would continue providing her transportation and paying her monthly bills. I, on the other hand, saw Galina as critical and bossy, resenting what I viewed as Galina's interference and unwanted advice. I was aware of her loneliness but had little sympathy for her and resented her dependency. The three of us struggled to work out a relationship.

To help relieve Galina's loneliness, I bought her a Chihuahua puppy. At first Galina was unsure about owning a dog and his arrival was greeted with mixed reviews. She named the puppy Poncho and before long was lavishing the pup with attention. Like most Chihuahuas, Poncho was very smart. He soon became bilingual, performing several tricks when asked in either Russian or English. Gradually, Galina adjusted to living on her own. Vic taught his mother how to write checks and pay her bills. I taught her how to drive and after much difficulty with the written portion of the driver's exam, she obtained her license. To celebrate, Vic took her car shopping. Soon Galina was driving herself to and from work. She loved her newfound independence.

With the arrival of our two daughters, tensions eased somewhat between Galina and me as she took on the role of grandmother. The girls called her Bobbie, short for Babushka, which is grandmother in Russian. The two loved spending the night at Bobbie's house. During their visits, the three usually went shopping for toys, books and clothes, all the things Galina had not been able to give her own son when he was growing up.

But despite having two granddaughters, the focus of Galina's world remained her son. Vic, aware of his mother's need for his attention, arranged to have a weekly luncheon with her, something they both enjoyed. These luncheons gave Galina the opportunity to prepare Vic's favorite dishes and she looked forward to having an hour of his undivided attention. Our family settled into a relationship with one another which was comfortable for all.

Looking back, I realize the onset of Galina's Alzheimer's Disease was very gradual, which is usually the case with this disease. Since Galina's native language was Russian, she often struggled to communicate in English. If a Russian speaker was in the room, she would turn to them asking, "How do you say...." if she didn't know the words. Because of this, when Galina had difficulty remembering words, lost track of appointments or forgot instructions, her difficulty was attributed to a poor command of English rather than to memory loss.

We first began to suspect Galina had a memory problem the day my husband came for his weekly visit and his mother wasn't at home. The doorbell went unanswered and finding the front door unlocked Vic grew concerned, fearing something had happened. He searched the house but found it empty. There were no signs that his mother had been preparing lunch except for the almost empty pan of water he found boiling on the stove. Turning off the gas, Vic sat down to await his mother's return. Galina, who had been out shopping, arrived several hours later to find a very upset son pacing the floor of her living room. When asked where she'd been and why she had missed their luncheon date, Galina became very defensive, claiming she thought he was coming tomorrow. Galina refused to believe she had left water boiling on her stove.

Concerned about the change in her behavior, we insisted Galina see her doctor for a complete checkup. I accompanied her, not trusting we would get an accurate report of his findings otherwise. After checking her thoroughly and ordering several tests, the doctor pronounced her fine. He dismissed concerns about her memory as, "just the normal changes due to old age." She was elated but I wasn't so sure there was no cause for concern.

The following year my husband and I decided to move to Tucson, Arizona, and open a tool store. Galina, not wanting to be separated from her family, agreed to move with us. One evening, shortly after our arrival in Tucson, we decided to see a movie. Galina declined our invitation to join us, preferring to stay at home and watch TV. When we returned, we found that she had decided to shampoo our area rugs– a nice idea in theory, but she had used the cleanser used on sinks rather than rug shampoo. She looked bewildered at our angry reaction as she had no idea why we were upset.

Despite her protests, I made an appointment for Galina to see a local doctor. During the examination, the physician gave her a simple mental examination. Galina's responses were mixed. She knew the President's name and also the month. She was less clear about where she was and could not count backward from 100 by 7's (something I find hard to do). When asked to remember three objects – a ball, a pear, and a car – and recall them a few minutes later, she failed miserably, unable to name a single one. The doctor agreed Galina had some memory problems but felt this was due to depression caused by her recent move from California. The doctor decided to treat her with antidepressants.

We had promised Galina we would build a cottage for her on the back of our property if she would move to Arizona with us. She wanted her own house furnished with her own things. Several months after her doctor's appointment, Galina's cottage was finished, and she and Poncho moved in. I hoped the memory problems would improve once Galina was surrounded by familiar belongings and the antidepressant began to work. Little did I know what lay ahead.

A few weeks after Galina moved into her cottage, I was shocked to receive a notice from the electric company threatening to shut off our power because our bill was two months overdue. A glance at my check-book showed they were correct. I hadn't written them a check for several months. I looked through the papers lying on my desk but couldn't find any electric bills among them. Mystified, I checked with Vic about the missing bill, but he was equally bewildered by its disappearance. On a hunch we decided to pay a visit to Galina's cottage. It didn't take long to discover a dresser drawer in her bedroom filled with our unopened mail. Letters, bills, throwaway ads – all were stuffed into the drawer. When questioning Galina, we discovered that while we were at work, Galina often walked down to the mailbox, collected our mail and squirreled it away. After a rather heated discussion, Galina tearfully agreed to leave the mail alone.

The next afternoon when I came home from work, I stopped to pick up our mail only to find the mailbox was empty. Suspicious, I paid a visit to the cottage and found our mail piled on Galina's dining room table. Frustrated, I asked why she had taken it. She gave me a confused look and denied she had touched the mail. Furious, I grabbed the envelopes and stomped out. This little drama was repeated many times over the next several months. Whenever the mail seemed to be missing, we headed to the cottage on a recovery mission. Bewildered, we couldn't understand why Galina kept taking our mail when we had repeatedly asked her to stop.

That fall I decided to go back to school and get a master's degree in nursing, something I had always wanted to do. One morning several months after I had begun my studies, I was standing in the hallway of the nursing building, waiting for an appointment with a professor who was running late. The gerontology professor, Dr. Porter, was in her office next door. The professor looked up, saw me standing in the hall and we began talking through her open doorway. I found myself telling Dr. Porter about my frustration with Galina, describing the disturbing behaviors she was exhibiting. "I just don't know what is wrong with her," I said in a voice which probably sounded like a wail. "She's driving me crazy." The professor, who had been listening intently, smiled sympathetically and said, "I can tell you what's wrong with your mother-in-law. She has Alzheimer's Disease." The professor went on to describe the disease and then gave me the name of a doctor she knew who specialized in geriatrics. The professor also offered me a book, *The 36-Hour Day* by Nancy L. Mace and Peter V. Rabins which she said would help me understand the disease. I started reading the book as soon as I got home, and I was amazed to see how Galina's behavior matched that of patients described in the book and how family members' reactions matched mine.

Without Dr. Porter's help, I don't know how much time would have passed before Galina's condition was diagnosed. In the 1980s, when these events occurred, information on Alzheimer's Disease was not readily available. Doctors were just learning about the disease, and few recognized Alzheimer's Disease in its early stages.

Once I had the information about Alzheimer's, I wasted no time getting help, and a week later Galina and I were sitting in Dr. Martin's office. Because Dr. Martin was a gerontologist, he was very familiar with the symptoms of Alzheimer's. Because of this knowledge, he spoke to Galina in a calm, sympathetic manner which she found very reassuring. After examining her and doing several tests, Dr. Martin confirmed the diagnosis. Sadly, Galina did indeed have Alzheimer's Disease

As I began to understand Alzheimer's effects on an individual, I realized I had to completely change my approach to managing Galina's behavior. The situation reminded me of when my daughters first started walking and getting into things. I knew they were incapable of understanding what might be dangerous or fragile, so instead of expecting them to know not to touch things that could break or be dangerous, I "baby-proofed" the house.

I became aware that I had to make that same kind of mental shift now. Instead of expecting my mother-in-law to change her disruptive behaviors, I needed to adjust her environment in such a way that the behaviors were prevented from occurring. It was time to get creative and to think outside the box. If I wanted Galina to stop collecting our mail, I needed to get a mailbox we could lock, one that could only be opened with a key. I mentally labeled the environmental adjustments we began making as "baby-proofing" the house. This mental shift from trying to control the person's behavior to changing his or her environment is often a difficult one for most caregivers to make.

Some of the incidents that occurred with Galina made us smile. One morning, my husband came in from cleaning the swimming pool, shaking his head. "I found a bunch of soggy bread floating in the pool skimmer" he said. "Do you have any idea where it came from?" I didn't have a clue, but a few days later we discovered Galina with a loaf of bread standing by the pool. She appeared transfixed by the sight of the pool sweep making its rounds. Casually, she broke off a piece of bread and threw it into the water. Apparently, she thought the pool sweep was some kind of animal and was feeding it bread like she had so often fed ducks in the past. Applying the "baby-proof the house" principal, Vic adjusted the timing of the pool sweep so it worked only at night when Galina wouldn't see it moving; problem solved. We were learning.

In the early stages of Galina's illness, she was aware she was having memory problems. She knew she remembered past events quite well but was unable to recall recent ones. This awareness was very stressful for her. She would become fearful and anxious, turning to me and saying, "Something is wrong with my head. Can you take me to the doctor so he can do something?" "We've been to the doctor, Galina," I would reply. "He is doing everything he can to help you." I can't imagine how frightening it must be not to be able to trust your memory. It seemed like a blessing when Galina's disease progressed to the stage where she was no longer aware of her memory lapses.

Galina enjoyed socializing with others, but since moving she had not had an opportunity to meet new people. We were at work or in school during the day and often were too busy at night and on weekends to spend much time with her. I was afraid her lack of social stimulation might be speeding up the progression of her disease. There was a Senior Center nearby which offered several activities I felt Galina would enjoy. I made arrangements for someone to drive her there each morning and I picked her up in the afternoon on my way home. Galina was delighted with this arrangement.

On Galina's first day, I walked into the center, curious to find out how her day had gone. Much to my surprise, I received very chilly greetings and several disapproving looks from the other seniors, a coolness which continued over the next several months. Mystified by their attitude, I kept wondering what I had done to offend them.

This question was answered a few months later. I was working at our tool store one morning when the phone rang. I answered and was surprised to hear Rita's voice. Rita was a friend of Galina's who lived in California. "Is this Joan?" she asked. When I replied it was, she sounded puzzled. "Are you at the store? How long have you been there?" "All morning," I replied. "Well," Rita said, "I'm confused. Galina just called me claiming you had just left her house. She said you were doing terrible things to her, hurting her. The things she said you were doing were awful. I was calling Vic to let him know about the abuse. I don't understand why she would say those awful things about you."

I explained to Rita about Galina Alzheimer's. "People with Alzheimer's can become paranoid and make up stories," I said. "It's just one of the symptoms of the disease." As I hung up the phone, I suddenly realized what was behind the cool reception I was receiving at the Senior Center. "Galina has been telling them stories," I thought. "No wonder I get dirty looks. It's a miracle someone hasn't called Adult Protective Services and reported me."

To my relief, the situation resolved itself in an unexpected way. Every Saturday Galina went to the beauty shop to get her hair done, something she loved to do. When I stopped by to drive Galina home, her beautician Maggie and I would chat as she finished working on Galina's hair. Maggie knew all about Galina's Alzheimer's and was very sympathetic, as her mother also suffered from the disease. One Saturday when picking Galina up from her appointment, I saw Gretchen, the woman who ran the Senior Center, sitting in the chair next to her. Gretchen looked surprised to see me. As Galina and I left the beauty shop, I looked back to wave goodbye to Maggie and saw her and Gretchen deep in conversation.

When I made my next visit to the Senior Center, I received a much warmer welcome. Several people even gave me hugs. Apparently, the conversation between Maggie and Gretchen had corrected Galina's misinformation. During the following months, these seniors continued to be loving and supportive.

Later I learned this type of behavior is very common among Alzheimer sufferers, especially when tension exists between patient and caregiver. Husbands are accused of being abusive or unfaithful; children, of stealing money. Fran, a woman I met at an Alzheimer's support group meeting, described her anger and frustration when her mother-in-law called Child Protective Services claiming Fran was abusing her children. "It took us a month to straighten out that mess," she sighed, "and to this day I still get questioning looks from some of my neighbors." Hearing her story made me feel more forgiving about my experience with Galina.

I confided to this group that listening to the countless repetition of questions like "Where are we going? Where are we going? Where are we going?" all day just wore me out. Another caregiver agreed, saying bluntly, "It drives me crazy when he asks the same question a hundred times. I want to just scream." Although no one had any suggestions about how to change the situation, talking to others who felt the same way somehow made me feel less guilty.

When Galina begin losing the ability to dress herself, I once again turned to the caregivers' group for suggestions. They introduced me to the concept of cuing. Cuing involves standing next to the Alzheimer's individuals and talking them through whatever task they are trying to perform, from brushing their teeth to getting dressed. Each morning, I would stand by Galina and give her hints such as "put your underpants on first," "put your foot through this opening," "now the other foot," "now pull up your pants." For a while cuing helped Galina remain somewhat independent. Eventually, the ability to follow instructions was lost and she needed someone to dress her

Time marched on, marked by Galina's gradual deterioration. One morning Gretchen called to tell me she felt the Senior Center was no longer an appropriate place for Galina. Galina was no longer able to participate in their activities and her behavior was making people uncomfortable. Gretchen suggested I look into the Day Care Program specifically designed for Alzheimer's patients, offered by Handmaker. I contacted Handmaker, a skilled nursing facility and a wonderful social worker by the name of Eileen came to evaluate Galina. As we sat talking, I told Eileen about the anger and frustration I felt when caring for Galina. "Maybe it would be different if she were my mother," I said, "but the two of us have never really gotten along. Sometimes I just lose it and end up yelling at her. I know she can't help being the way she is, but it can be so frustrating."

I can still see the compassionate look on Eileen face as she said, "Everyone finds caring for someone with Alzheimer's terribly hard. All the characteristics the person had before they became ill seem to intensify with the disease. If your mother-in-law felt antagonistic toward you before her illness, she feels it much more deeply now. Don't feel guilty;

you and your husband are doing a lot more than most people do." "I really needed to hear that," I told her gratefully.

Daycare was a Godsend. Galina went every day from 10 to 4. Along with socialization and memory games, the center also offered personal care: bathing, cutting toe and fingernails, along with a hot lunch at noon. Many people with Alzheimer's develop a fear of water, making bathing very difficult for them. Showering had become a real battleground for us and having the daycare take over this responsibility was a huge relief. Everyone happily settled into our new routine, which lasted for several years.

As Galina's disease progressed, so did her paranoia. She became fearful at night and began experiencing "sundowners" syndrome. Sundowners refers to an increase in the agitation, confusion and restlessness many Alzheimer's patients experience around sunset. Because of sundowners, Galina became convinced people were trying to break into her cottage. One morning Vic discovered black streaks along a wall by the electrical sockets where Galina had tried to stick safety pins into the socket to pin the edges of her bedroom drapes shut believing intruders were outside. It was obvious it was no longer safe for her to stay alone. We needed to find a place where she could receive the care she needed.

In Tucson, there are a number of people who run private group homes which provide live-in care to people who are no longer able to live independently. Vic and I began visiting these homes, feeling that for Galina, this situation was preferable to a skilled nursing facility. After one unsuccessful placement, we found the perfect situation. It was a beautifully kept home supervised by an LPN named Marilyn. In addition to caring for her own mother, who had died of Alzheimer's Disease, Marilyn had studied the condition extensively, attending numerous workshops and conferences. Feeling she had learned all she could about the disease, Marilyn decided to open a group home for women with the ailment. She employed several additional caregivers whom she carefully trained, and they too became skilled in managing Alzheimer's behaviors. After a thorough assessment of Galina's social behaviors, Marilyn agreed to admit Galina to her care home.

On my first visit, I found a much more relaxed Galina sitting in the yard with a contented look on her face watching a 2-year-old little girl, the daughter of one of the caregivers, toddling around the garden and being chased by her puppy. Much to our delight, it soon became obvious that Galina was much happier here than she had been living at home. No one had any expectations about how she "should" behave, and she was somehow aware of this, which accounted for her more relaxed demeanor.

Because Galina liked keeping busy, the staff let her set the table and help in the kitchen before meals. During our visits she would proudly announce she had to go to work now and trot off to the kitchen. She felt useful and totally accepted and loved.

Marilyn seldom took her ladies on outings, feeling that strange environments were disturbing to her charges. Instead, she had several people come to the home. Once a week a beautician came to do everyone's hair. Another woman came several times a month and provided manicures and pedicures. A class of fourth graders from the nearby grade school adopted these forgetful "grandmothers" and dropped by frequently to visit and bring the elders pictures they had drawn. Galina's gerontologist stopped by once a month to check on everyone and adjust medications as needed.

At some point in the progression of Alzheimer's, the disease begins to affect the appetite, either causing the person to eat all the time or to lose their appetite almost completely. Aware of this, Marilyn weighed her charges weekly. She became concerned when she noticed Galina had begun to lose weight. Marilyn began investigating and soon discovered the cause of Galina's weight loss: it was Helen. Helen and Galina were inseparable, sharing a room and sitting together during meals. Helen was always starving and Galina, who no longer found food appealing, was sneaking her food onto Helen's plate where it quickly disappeared. While Galina was losing weight, Helen was rapidly gaining unwanted pounds. Marilyn quietly found ways to separate the two at meals. In addition, she started Galina on Ensure, which became her major source of nutrition for the next few years.

As their disease progresses, individuals lose their ability to understand words. Instead, the Alzheimer sufferer uses the tone of voice, facial expressions and body language as clues in order to understand what is going on. Does the speaker look happy? Mad? Sad? Because of this inability to process language, it is important to keep one's voice low and one's expression pleasant. The higher the pitch of the voice, the angrier the tone, the tenser the body language, the more agitated the person will become. Although I knew I needed to retain a calm demeanor with Galina, I had found this very difficult to remember when Galina resisted doing something, I felt was necessary for her to do, like bathing or taking medications. But Marilyn had mastered the art of always maintaining her cool.

One morning I sat watching as Marilyn refused to let Galina use a knife to cut up vegetables. Marilyn kept her tone patient, reasonable and calm as she talked to Galina. Rather than arguing with her, Marilyn simply diverted Galina's attention from the knife by asking if she would mind washing the dishes. With her memory loss, Galina promptly forgot all about the knife once something else caught her attention. Diversion proved to be a great strategy in dealing with Alzheimer behaviors, one Marilyn and her crew used often.

I felt so grateful we had found this place for Galina. I knew I was incapable of giving Galina the loving care and understanding she needed. What a relief to know I had found people who could. During some of our visits, we would take Galina on outings. We soon discovered going

51

to restaurants no longer worked. Galina's table manners had deteriorated to the point where she ate foods like mashed potatoes with her hands. Although we found this embarrassing when other diners looked at her aghast, the real clincher came at the end of the meal. Galina would finish eating and then begin stuffing her purse with the sugar bowl, silverware, salt and pepper shakers or anything else that wasn't nailed down. She became enraged when we told her she could not take these "treasures" home with her. So instead of going to restaurants, we began taking her to the park for picnics. We would pick up a bucket of her favorite fried chicken dinner and head out. Galina loved watching other families with their children sitting at nearby tables and no one minded if she ate with her hands. She was encouraged to take home all the plastic knives and forks she wanted, "the baby-proofing the house" principle once more in action.

As Galina's condition deteriorated, she became reluctant to leave Marilyn's which she now regarded as home. One Christmas morning we brought Galina to our house to spend the day. Realizing her mental capacity had greatly deteriorated, I had chosen gifts one might give a child: a soft, furry, stuffed mother cat with two kittens and a child's picture book of animals. She was delighted with her presents, rubbing the cat's soft fur against her face. An hour after her arrival, however, Galina demanded to go home. "But we haven't had dinner," I protested. Ignoring me or more probably not understanding what I was saying, she kept repeating, "I want to go home, I want to go home," her agitation gradually increasing. Sadly, we loaded her into the car and took her back to Marilyn's, realizing another chapter had ended. Galina would no longer be celebrating holidays at our house.

During our next visit Galina suddenly turned to Vic and said, "Have you seen Victor lately? I haven't seen him in ages." I can still remember the stunned look on my husband's face and the tears he tried to hold back as he realized his mother no longer knew who he was. "Yes, I've seen Victor," my husband replied gamely. "He's doing great." After our visit,

I turned to Vic and said, "At this stage, it's really up to you how often you want to visit. I can see it really hurts you to see her like this. Five minutes after we leave, she doesn't remember we were there. But you, you remember the visit and how she looks for days." After that discussion, we cut back on the frequency of visits to Galina. I realized Vic just needed permission to stop going so often.

Toward the last stage of Alzheimer's individuals become incontinent. This problem is not due to any deterioration in their bodily functioning. Rather it is due to the fact the person is unable to recognize their body's signals indicating they need to urinate or have a bowel movement. At first this incontinence can be managed by taking the individual to the bathroom on a regular schedule, every two hours or so. As time goes on, this strategy no longer works, and diapers are needed. Marilyn called one morning to say Galina had reached the diaper stage and she needed our permission to charge them to our monthly bill. Permission we gladly gave. I also knew Galina's incontinence was a sign her deterioration was accelerating.

I received a call from Marilyn several months later. When the aide had gone to get Galina washed up for breakfast, she found Galina was unable to walk. She could move her legs but when the aide attempted to help her stand, Galina promptly collapsed. This loss of the ability to stand or walk occurs in the final stage of Alzheimer's. Galina had simply forgotten how.

One of the state regulations for care homes is that residents must be able to walk and cannot be bed bound or wheelchair bound. The state regulators feel these individuals require more care than can be provided by a care home. Galina would have to be moved.

Galina had grown considerably weaker. She was barely drinking Ensure, had lost considerable weight and now had lost her ability to walk. "Maybe," I thought, "she might be a candidate for the hospice inpatient unit." I contacted the hospice office which sent out a nurse to evaluate Galina's condition. Shortly after her visit, the nurse made arrangements for Galina to be admitted to hospice.

Once she was moved to her room in hospice, Galina seemed to relax and settle into the business of dying. She was very weak and spent much of her time sleeping. Even though Galina no longer recognized me, I felt the need to say a private goodbye to her. One afternoon when I knew we would be alone, I went to her room and sat in the chair next to her bed. I closed my eyes and pictured the two of us sitting talking. I realized as I sat there that without Galina's presence in my life, I would have skipped along believing I was little Mary Sunshine, all sweetness and light. The angry clashes between Galina and me had left me with feelings of anger, jealousy and at times a thirst for revenge. These intense emotions were quickly followed by feelings of guilt. I had spent years trying to convince myself that if Galina wasn't so difficult to be around, I wouldn't be this terrible person, having these horrible unacceptable feelings.

With maturity came the realization that these feelings were a part of me, part of who I am. My interactions with Galina had provided a means for surfacing these emotions so I could no longer pretend this shadowy part of myself didn't exist. Because of our interactions, I had learned to recognize and deal with these emotions rather than letting them overwhelm and control me. As I sat by Galina's bedside, I was filled with a sense of gratitude as I realized Galina had been one of my greatest teachers. I quietly thanked her for all she had given me and asked her to forgive me for the times I had been unkind. I left her room feeling our differences had been resolved.

Shortly before her death, Vic and I were sitting at her bedside one evening when Galina suddenly opened her eyes. I looked at her and saw she was there, the eyes that had looked at us blankly for years were suddenly filled with intelligence. She looked at Vic and said, "Victor, I love you." This was the first time she had ever said those words to him. He was astonished. Then she turned to me and said, "Joanie, Paseba" which is Russian for thank you. Slowly the light faded from her eyes and the intelligence left her face and the real her was no longer there. Amazing. It had been at least three years since Galina had recognized us or spoken intelligibly to anyone. I realized then that underneath all those tangled neurons in her brain, Galina remained alive and intact. I don't know what the effort to come say goodbye to us cost her, but I shall forever be grateful to her for making it.

Very early the next morning the phone rang. It was the hospice nurse informing us that Galina was actively dying. The nurse told us if we wanted to be with her, we had to hurry because things were changing rapidly, and we didn't have much time. Vic, our daughter Nicole and I threw on our clothes and rushed across town to the hospital. We dashed into Galina's room and found her unresponsive but still breathing. The three of us put our arms around her and told her we loved her as her breathing slowly stopped. What felt like a light breeze lifted from her and went on its way and she was gone. The nurse stepped into the room, took in the scene and said, "She really must have wanted you with her. I didn't think you would get here in time, but she held on and waited for you."

Afterthoughts

Shortly after Galina's death, I was asked to be on a panel. The panel was part of a conference on Alzheimer's for both caregivers and medical staff. During the discussion I was asked, "What was the hardest part of caring for your mother-in-law?" My response surprised me. Without thinking I immediately replied, "Dealing with my guilt, my guilt about all the times I was angry and impatient with her," I added. The questioner looked startled; this was not the answer he was expecting. Looking out

55

at the audience, I saw a number of people nodding, identifying with my answer. I knew immediately who the caregivers in that audience were.

The lessons I learned caring for Galina were extremely valuable ones, ones I often used when working with Alzheimer's families in my nursing practice, especially the "baby-proofing the house" principle. I will never forget the day I received a phone call from Hazel, the sole caregiver for her husband Harry, who had the disease. She called me in tears. "I just had to talk to someone who would understand," she said. "I am so upset with Harry; I could just kill him." Unbeknownst to Hazel, Harry had decided to go out to the garage and work on their car. Although Hazel kept the car locked, her husband had found his car keys, unlocked the car door and popped open the lid to the gas tank. For some reason known only to Harry, he had picked up the funnel he used when adding oil, inserted it into the gas tank and began pouring in sugar he had brought from the pantry. It cost me over five hundred dollars to get the car fixed," Hazel sobbed. "I can't afford to keep doing that. When I tried to take his keys away from him, he became so upset I gave up. I don't know what to do."

Following the "baby-proofing the house" principle, I suggested she take the keys when her husband was asleep and file down the grooves with a rasp; a suggestion she promptly carried out. Several days later she reported with a great deal of relief that Harry had made several trips to the garage to work on the car, only to return a few minutes later saying he didn't know why, but his key just wouldn't unlock the car door. Eventually he gave up trying. Problem solved.

I have often wondered if there is any greater purpose to having Alzheimer's. I met a Professor of Nursing from Minnesota who had an interesting theory regarding why individuals develop certain diseases. She felt the diseases an individual develops are part of a person's life pattern through which everyone's spiritual development is advanced. Hearing her theory made me look at Galina's illness in a different way.

Throughout Galina's life, she was not able to accept love. When we told her we loved her, we could almost feel the love we were giving bounce back off the hard, protective shell she had formed around herself. As her Alzheimer's advanced, this shell disappeared, and she could at last accept love from the people who surrounded her. She seemed to soak it up like a very dry sponge soaking up water. Was learning to accept love one of the purposes of Galina's Alzheimer's? I don't pretend to know, but I find it comforting to think having the disease might have served some greater purpose in Galina.

SANDRA

Not understanding the dying process can cause needless guilt.

I recently had an opportunity to make use of some of the knowledge I have gained through the years, when I reconnected with my friend Sandra. I had not seen Sandra for at least ten years. During that time her husband Larry had died. The couple were very close and after they both retired, they did everything together. Each summer they planted a huge garden where they enjoyed working side by side. They loved cooking together and the couple was famous for the spaghetti sauce they made from tomatoes grown in their garden as well as their sweet pickles which had won prizes at several county fairs.

Despite their closeness, Larry was a very undemonstrative husband and father. Although Larry loved telling jokes and giving gifts, he seldom hugged or kissed his wife and daughter. Showing or expressing emotions seemed beyond his capabilities.

As Sandra and I sat talking, catching up on the past ten years, Sandra began telling me about Larry's death, saying, "Something happened just before Larry died that I just haven't been able to get over." Sandra went on to described how she spent the last few days before her husband's death at Larry's bedside. One morning shortly before he died, her husband seemed unusually alert. Sensing their time together was nearly gone, Sandra had taken Larry's hand and had told him how much she loved him and how much she was going to miss him. She sat waiting for his response. Several minutes passed. Larry had simply laid there looking at her for a long moment, then he closed his eyes and turned away without saying a word. She began to cry as she related the story, saying she, felt Larry must have been angry with her or that she had done something wrong. "How could he die without saying a word to me? Without telling me he loved me?"

Sandra, who has always suffered from a feeling of insecurity, immediately interpreted Larry's failure to respond as proof that she had not been a good wife and that Larry had never really loved her. Unable to get over these destructive feelings, Sandra said she gone to see a counselor.

"Did that help?" I asked. "It made things worse," Sandra replied. She went on to explain that when she told the counselor what had happened the counselor responded by telling this poor woman that her husband's behavior showed he must have been very angry with her to have refused to talk to her when he knew he was dying. "The counselor also told me I must have had a terrible marriage," Sandra said, by this time sobbing openly. "And I needed to work on all the pent-up anger I felt towards Larry."

Putting aside my homicidal feelings towards any counselor who would say something like this to a grieving widow, I gave Sandra a hug and waited until her crying stopped. Then I began talking. I started by reassuring Sandra her husband's reaction was not unusual, that some people are simply unable to express their emotions. I asked Sandra how Larry had reacted when their daughter was born. "He loved holding Darcy," Sandra replied, a smile crossing her face as she remembered a happier time. "Darcy was a colicky baby and Larry would walk her for hours whenever she cried," Sandra recalled. "Did he ever say he loved Darcy?" I asked. "No," Sandra said, looking thoughtful. "But I could tell from the way he acted how he felt about her." "So, you can see how difficult it was for Larry to express his feelings," I replied.

"You could tell Larry loved you, Sandra," I continued. "You could see how he felt about you by the way he treated you. But when he was dying, I don't think he knew how to express what he was feeling without becoming emotional and crying, something he would never allow himself to do." Sandra looked thoughtful.

"Were you with Larry when he died?" I asked. "No," said Sandra. "I had stepped into the hall for just a few minutes to answer a call from Darcy and when I came back Larry was gone. I felt terrible about that. I feel like he didn't want me with him when he died." Once again tears welled up in Sandra's eyes.

I told Sandra about the many times I had seen this happen over the years I was working for hospice and the reasons I felt this happened. "Because you two were so close, it was just too hard for Larry to let go when you were sitting next to him," I suggested. "So, he waited until you were gone." A look of relief swept over Sandra's face as she began to understand what I was saying. Sandra, beginning to sound a little angry, said, "My therapist told me that Larry chose to die when I wasn't with him because he was angry with me. " I didn't know how to respond so I just sat there listening, shaking my head no.

As we continued to talk, I could tell Sandra was beginning to understand that Larry's behavior towards her was not a sign he was angry but rather that he simply didn't know how to express his feelings. Tears welled up in Sandra's eyes as she said, "That poor dear man, it must have been so hard to have all that loved trapped inside with no way to let it out." As she said this, I could see Sandra grow more relaxed as she let go of the hurt and the anger she had been holding so tightly inside.

Although Sandra's feelings about Larry's death were beginning to dissipate, I knew how strong her tendency toward harsh self-criticism was. Fearing her old feelings might reoccur, I suggested Sandra call a local hospice and join one of their bereavement groups. Bereavement counselors, with their in-depth knowledge of the dying process, are especially skillful at helping survivors work through the variety of emotional issues that can occur after the death of a loved one.

It's hard to believe for me to believe that the counselor Sandra worked with actually said the harsh things Sandra reported. It is possible that the therapist said something very different and because of Sandra's strong sense of rejection and guilt, Sandra put her own interpretation on her counselor's words. In any case, I strongly recommended to Sandra that if she felt she needed a counselor in the future, she finds a new one.

When it was time to go, I told Sandra how sorry I was she had gone through such a traumatic experience. Sandra gave me one final hug, and said with a smile, "You have no idea how much talking with you has helped. I am so grateful. Next time I go to Mass I am going to light a candle for you." We promised to stay in touch and as I walked away, I found myself praying that Sandra had found some peace at last.

Afterthoughts

Each person grieves in their own time and in their own way. My daughters are a reminder of how true this is. When Nicole suffers a loss, begins to experience grief almost immediately. She cries freely and feels tearful and sad much of the time. This stage which can last up to a year, slowly recedes and she goes on with her life with only an occasional return of tears.

In contrast, Anne's initial reaction to a loss is to show little or no emotion. She lets her grief out in little spurts. Several weeks after the loss occurs, something will trigger her grief and Anne will have a few teary days and then quickly return to her usual self. Several months later something else will trigger her grief and the teary days return. This cycle often goes on for several years as she works through her feelings surrounding her loss. My grief process is similar to Anne's.

Children of widowed mothers or fathers often criticize their parent for not moving through their grief fast enough saying, "For heaven's sake Mom, Dad's been gone for months. Why are you still crying? You need to get over it." It's hard for others to understand what the loss of someone you love means to you emotionally.

Certain "anniversary" dates such as birthdays, wedding anniversaries, or the date the death occurred can trigger our grief. For several years I could not understand why I became so sad around Thanksgiving. Then one year I suddenly remembered that my father had died a week after the holiday. Now that I know Thanksgiving is a trigger for me, I can accept the fact I am going to feel "a little blue" for a few days and move on.

61

Families of someone who dies after a long illness, often find themselves experiencing grief before the death occurs. This is called anticipatory grieving. Although these family members feel a sense of loss when the loved one's death finally happens, there is also a sense of relief that the ailing individual is no longer suffering. Our family certainly experienced this with Galina's death.

When death occurs suddenly, without warning, the initial reaction is often a sense of disbelief and shock. Gradually this numbness begins to melt away and the ability to feel returns. It is then, several months later that the survivor begins to feel the emotional impact of their loss.

It is not unusual for survivors to see their loved one or hear their voice after they are gone. Sometimes the loved one returns in vivid dreams. I often feel my Dad's presence, particularly in times of stress, and it is comforting to have him with me.

Most hospices offer bereavement groups which are open to anyone who has experienced a loss. Because of the huge emotional ups and downs that occur after a death, it is easy to feel our reactions are abnormal. As one of the survivors I worked with put it, "I thought I was going crazy one day, when I found myself standing in the produce section of the grocery store crying. I was buying green beans and they were one of my husband's favorites. How stupid. Who cries over green beans?" The bereavement group assured her that this was perfectly normal. Many of them had experienced the same sort of thing.

Often survivors find seeing others who are finding the strength to rebuild their lives very helpful. As one put it, "Hearing a woman in our group talk about a cruise she was planning to take with a friend, made me realize that someday my life would be good again."

Grieving is hard, but necessary, work. Be kind to yourself and accept the fact that you have the right to be sad for as long as you need to feel that way. If you are struggling, reach out to others and let them know you need help. Just know that with time, grief eventually does subside, and life does get better.

DAN AND BETH

Helpers often appear to assist us as we make our transition.

I met Dan Parson, his wife Beth and their four children in 1960, shortly after I moved to California. Beth had grown up in Seattle and Dan in Minnesota. After graduating from high school, Dan joined the Navy. While stationed in Seattle he met Beth and after a week-long courtship they were married.

Although Dan's mother Estelle had two sons, Estelle made it clear to everyone that Dan was her favorite. She doted on Dan and expected him to return to Minnesota once his tour of duty was finished. Estelle was furious when she learned Dan had married. When she met Dan's new bride, she took an instant dislike to Beth and constantly criticized her daughter-in-law to anyone who would listen, often in Beth's presence. Dan, aware of his mother's behavior, found it difficult to confront her. When his parents came for a visit, Dan avoided the conflict by working extra-long hours, leaving Beth to cope with Estelle's hostility on her own.

One day shortly before Christmas, I got a phone call from Beth. Dan's parents were arriving in a couple of days to spend the holidays with them. Knowing Estelle's presence was going to dampen everyone's Christmas spirits, Beth was dreading their visit. To cheer herself up, Beth had decided to spend the day relaxing and writing Christmas cards before she plunged into the work of getting ready for her in-law's visit. When she invited me to join her, I happily agreed to come.

Late that afternoon Beth and I were just finishing the last of our cards when the phone rang. It was Dan calling to tell Beth that his parents had decided to surprise them by arriving three days early and that the couple would be at the Parson's home in an hour. Beth hung up the phone, panic written across her face. "Look at this mess," she cried, glancing around the living room, which was strewn with the day's accumulation of toys, clothes and other miscellaneous items. The kitchen was also a disaster with unwashed breakfast and lunch dishes stacked in the sink and honey dribbling down the counter. As Beth and I stood surveying the messy house, the front door opened and four dirty, wet kids fresh from playing in mud puddles tromped inside. Beth looked at me in despair. "If Estelle sees the house looking like this, I'll never hear the end of it. It's all she'll talk about for years. What am I going to do?"

I took a deep breath. "Don't worry, we can figure this out," I said. "You take care of cleaning the kitchen and getting dinner, the kids and I will take care of the rest." Following my instructions, the children and I quickly grabbed armloads of clutter from the floor and furniture and stuffed everything out of sight under their beds. When we had finished picking up, the children showered and dressed in their pajamas while I vacuumed and dusted the house and cleaned the bathrooms. Together the kids and I readied the guest bedroom.

Meanwhile, Beth loaded the dishwasher, cleaned the kitchen and set the table. Finding a roast in the freezer, she popped it into the oven along with carrots and potatoes. With fresh makeup, a change of clothes and her hair neatly combed, Beth looked prepared for anything, even Estelle. The two of us had just poured ourselves a glass of wine when we heard a car driving up. It was Dan coming from the train station where he had picked up his parents. A minute later, the front door opened, and the guests arrived.

I wish I had a picture that captured Estelle's expression when she walked into the house. It was obvious she had hoped to catch Beth in a state of disarray. Disappointment tinged with disbelief flitted across her face as Estelle took in the spotless house and the four freshly bathed grandchildren sitting in their pajamas smiling at her. Dan could not hide his relief. This tranquil scene was accentuated by the aroma of roast beef wafting in from the kitchen. Beth and I couldn't look at one another for fear we would burst out laughing at the way we had outmaneuvered Estelle. From this moment on, Beth and I became more like sisters than good friends, lending one another a helping hand whenever needed.

One morning several years later, I got a phone call from Beth. She sounded distraught and asked if I could come right over. When I arrived,

I found her in tears. "Last week I noticed a mole on Dan's back was bleeding," she said. "I finally convinced him to have our doctor take a look at it. Dr. Bradley just called to say the biopsy report came back positive. Dan's mole is cancerous, a melanoma. He wants Dan to see a surgeon and have another biopsy to see if the cancer has spread. God, I am so scared. If anything happens to Dan, I don't know what I'll do." I sat with my friend feeling helpless, listening to her fears, unable to find words to comfort her.

The second biopsy report was the worst possible news. Dan's cancer had spread to his lymph nodes and would ultimately spread throughout his body. Chemotherapy and radiation were ineffective against this type of cancer. There was no cure. Dan and Beth were stunned. Dan was only 37. How could something like this happen? The doctor had no answers to the couple's questions regarding how much time Dan had or what to expect next. He merely shook his head, saying, "We'll just have to wait and see."

Several years went by and to everyone's amazement, Dan seemed perfectly fine. He coped with the uncertainty of his health status by working even longer hours and drinking late into the night with his buddies. Beth resented the time Dan spent away from home, feeling their remaining time was precious and Dan should be spending it at home with his family. She was also very frightened. Not only would she be left to raise four children on her own when Dan was gone, but she had no idea how she would support them. The couple had no life insurance, and Beth, who had never worked outside the home, had no job skills. Dan had tried to start a business several years before, which had not only failed but had wiped out their savings. What was she going to do? Unlike Dan, Beth coped with her anxiety with denial, pretending everything was normal and trying not to think about what might lie ahead. As the months passed and there were no visible changes in Dan's condition, family and friends grew hopeful that somehow a miracle had taken place and Dan was cured.

Reality came crashing in one night when Dan woke up with severe abdominal pain. A trip to the Emergency Room revealed his melanoma had spread to his abdomen, causing a bowel obstruction. Surgery was performed to relieve the obstruction, but it was clear the cancer was on the move. That night, an exhausted Beth agreed to go home to her children, provided I spend the night at the hospital with Dan. Dan was awake but didn't feel like talking. Instead he spent the night staring at the ceiling not saying a word. I sat silently in the darkened hospital room watching Dan fight sleep while he tried to absorb the realization that his hope had just been shattered.

Dan recovered quickly from his surgery and was soon back at work. Dan's boss, a very compassionate man, offered to continue to pay Dan's salary and provide medical insurance to Dan and his family for as long as Dan lived, regardless of his ability to work, an offer Dan gratefully accepted. As the weeks passed, Dan's priorities began to change. He began working fewer hours and spending more time at home with Beth and his children.

Over the next several months, Dan's condition gradually worsened. He continued to work for as long as he was physically able, at first shortening his hours, finally having to quit working altogether. He was experiencing pain and needed morphine injections to relieve his discomfort. The year was 1972, before hospice care was available in this country. Since their health insurance did not cover the cost of private nursing care, it was up to Beth and the children to provide the help Dan needed. I taught the family how to give his morphine injections and ways to make Dan comfortable. After contacting several agencies, the Visiting Nurse Association agreed to send a nurse's aide twice a week to assist with Dan's personal care.

Jackie, a friend of Beth's, also offered to help. Together the two of us worked out a plan to provide Beth with some much-needed respite by making weekly visits. During our visits Jackie and Beth went out to lunch while I stayed with Dan.

I began to look forward to my visits with Dan. As he grew weaker, he no longer had the energy to put up his usual "tough guy" defenses and began expressing thoughts and emotions he normally kept hidden. A friend once described this process like this: "As the overcoat grows thinner, one can see the spirit shining through." Dan's spirit was starting to glow. He became very introspective, expressing regret that he had made work rather than family his priority. "Until recently, I barely knew my kids," he confided one day, "I was so focused on work I didn't make time for anything else. The only good thing that has come out of this whole mess is that I've gotten a chance to really know them. They are great kids. I only wish I was going to be around to see them grow up," he added sadly.

Dan also shared his fears about dying and his concerns about his family, topics he felt Beth would find too painful. Dan was very aware of Beth's emotional fragility and how hard she was struggling not to let their situation overwhelm her emotionally. He knew Beth and the children needed more time to develop the inner strength necessary to cope with his leaving, and he was doing his best to give it to them.

Each of the children reacted to Dan's illness in a different way. Susie, at 19, was midway through her first year of college. Shortly before Christmas, she eloped with her college sweetheart, dropped out of school and soon became pregnant. Riley who was 17 and the oldest child still living at home, became his mother's stalwart supporter, learning to give morphine injections and helping with Dan's care. Davy, the youngest, had just turned 13. He refused to discuss his father's illness and spent long hours alone in his room.

Lily, the spunky one, was 15 and in her sophomore year of high school when Dan's illness reached its final stage. Furious that her father was dying, Lily began skipping school, drinking and staying out after curfew. Since Dan had always been the disciplinarian, Beth had no idea how to handle the situation and resented Lily's acting out which only added to Beth's already loaded plate of emotional distress. "How can she behave this way when her Dad's so sick?" Beth would wonder. "Doesn't she know how bad it makes him feel to see her act like this when he is too weak to stop her? Aren't we going through enough without her adding to it?" Dan's attempts to talk to Lily only made her angrier and resulted in her stomping out of the house.

One day as Dan and I sat talking, I could sense there was something important he wanted to discuss but was hesitant to bring the subject up. Finally, Dan looked at me and said, "I want to tell you something, but I am afraid you are going to think I'm crazy." I looked at him curiously, wondering what he was about to say. "I keep seeing a pink penguin," he said with a sheepish grin. "A what?" I asked, astonished, not sure Dan, who was a great tease, wasn't regaling me with some tall tale. "A pink penguin," he repeated, shaking his head. "At first, I only saw him when I was dreaming, but lately I am seeing him when I am awake. Isn't that crazy?"

Realizing Dan was serious, I began asking questions. "What does the penguin do? Does he say anything?" "Sometimes he talks to me," Dan replied. "But the thing is, when he appears, I don't know how to describe it." Dan looked thoughtful for a moment. "I feel so peaceful, like everything is going to be all right." Then, as though he felt like our discussion was becoming too serious, Dan started to chuckle. "You know, I have always been a pretty heavy drinker; if I was going to start seeing things, you'd think it would be pink elephants, not penguins." We both laughed.

The pink penguin became a sort of running joke between Dan and me, and during each visit I got an update on Dan's further adventures with his new friend. The penguin not only brought a sense of peace to Dan but told him what was important for him to say to each of his children and to Beth before he died. It wasn't until much later when I began working in hospice that I understood the penguin's significance.

Beth was becoming emotionally stronger, developing the inner strength she so badly needed to let Dan go. We knew time was running out as we watched Dan grow steadily weaker, but when his death finally occurred it caught us all by surprise. As Susie put it, "I knew my dad would die someday. I just didn't expect it to be today."

When Beth called to tell me Dan had died, she said, "I feel so guilty that I wasn't with him. I was just so tired. I had been up all night with Dan; he was restless and couldn't settle down. Today he kept asking for things – rub his feet, fluff his pillow – I was just so tired. Finally, I told him I had to go into the other room and take a nap. Susie and her husband were here, and they agreed to stay with him while I rested. I told him to please, just let me rest for an hour without any interruptions. I was sound asleep when Susie woke me and told me he had died."

Because the family had no money for a funeral, Dan had donated his body to Stanford University. He also made Beth promise not to have a memorial service, a request his family and friends found difficult to carry out. Without a service, we were denied the opportunity to celebrate Dan's life and to say our goodbyes. It felt so empty, doing nothing. This was especially hard for Dan's children.

The family had some difficult years after Dan's death, adjusting to the changes in their lives. Beth sold the house and rented an apartment. The money from the sale supported the family long enough for the children to finish high school. All four grew up to be caring adults who went on to have successful careers and raise wonderful families. Dan would have been very proud of them.

Eventually Beth remarried and fifty-eight years later, we remain close friends. My husband Vic and I are an adopted aunt and uncle to Dan's children. When we have "family reunions" we often reminisce about Dan and our times together, the good times together with the painful ones.

Afterthoughts

I did not understand the significance of Dan's pink penguin until I started working in hospice. The appearance of some type of being like the penguin is quite common among dying individuals, and their purpose seems to be to lessen fears and to help ease the transition between this world and whatever comes next. Frequently the "visitor" is a deceased family member, close friend or a beloved pet. Sometimes people see a spiritual figure like Jesus. The Virgin Mary visits many people, especially Catholics. She is described as a beautiful golden lady and usually sits in a chair by the bedside of a dying individual. Whenever I come to see someone who is dying, I have learned to ask permission before sitting down to make sure the chair where I intend to sit is empty.

Children can often see these "beings." I will always remember my experience with Amy, a lively four-year-old granddaughter of one of my patients. Amy was vising her grandmother when I stopped by one afternoon. When she heard my knock, she ran to open the door and gave me an enthusiastic greeting. "What have you and your grandmother been doing today?" I asked her. The little girl gave me a big grin and said in a very matter-of-fact tone, "I've been sitting in bed with grandma talking to the lady on the wall." Sure enough, when I went in to see Amy's grandmother, she confirmed what Amy had told me; a beautiful golden lady was indeed visiting the pair. Although unexpected, I was not surprised when Amy's grandmother died peacefully several weeks later.

I am by nature a "doubting Thomas." Although I kept hearing about these presences during my hospice visits, there was still a part of me that doubted their existence. Gladys, a sweet little eighty-four-year old, provided me with additional proof of their validity. When I came to see her one morning, her two daughters met me at the door. "I don't know what has gotten into Mother today," Elena the oldest said. "She has been snapping our heads off all morning."

"That's not like her," I agreed. "Maybe she's having more pain. Why don't you two stay here while I go talk to her," I suggested.

Gladys looked up as I came in. "Gladys, the girls tell me you are having a bad morning," I began. "What's going on?" "I'm just so angry with my daughters," Gladys replied. "Last night I started sort of drifting back and forth between here and the other side like I have been doing lately. While I was over there, I saw Mary, my older sister. She's dead. She said she decided to go first and help me make the journey. My sister died and my girls didn't even have the decency to tell me."

When I returned to where the girls sat anxiously waiting, I told them what Gladys had said. They looked stricken. "My cousin John called last night to tell us his mother had a heart attack and died very suddenly," Elena explained. "We thought about telling Mom, but Mom's so close to dying herself we felt there was no point in upsetting her. I guess we were wrong. We'll go in and straighten things out with her."

Although many individuals are visited by friends, family members or religious figures such as Jesus or Mary, in retrospect it made perfect sense to me that Dan would experience a pink penguin. While in the Navy, Dan had spent time in Korea. While there, he had observed missionaries offering rice to the starving population on the condition they became Christians. This experience left Dan feeling bitter toward all religions, particularly Christianity. He would not have tolerated the appearance of any type of religious figure and he had no close relationship with any deceased family or friends. A pink penguin was just outlandish enough to appeal to his sense of humor, slip past his defenses and help ease him through his dying process.

The appearance of these beings is not only comforting to the one whose life is ending but to their families as well. Families of these individuals no longer feel their loved one is going away into nothingness but instead feel their loved one is being accompanied by someone or something the dying person knows and who cares about him or her. As one spouse put it, "Knowing Everett is with his sister is such a comfort. The two were always close and he was so pleased when she came to him as he was dying. It makes it easier somehow."

After years of hospice nursing, I look back on my experience with Dan and realize there are two things I would have suggested Dan and his family do. The first suggestion would be for Dan to write letters to Beth and to each of his children, telling them how much they meant to him and his hopes for their future. This would have given them a tangible message from Dan that they could hold on to after he was gone.

I now realize how much a small memorial service, an informal gathering of family and friends, would have helped everyone who loved Dan to express their grief and achieve a sense of closure. Denied this opportunity, several of Dan's children, with the help of their therapists, eventually found ways to experience their individual closures by writing farewell letters to Dan or holding their own personal memorials. My experience has taught me how important it is to remember that funerals and memorial services are not held for the benefit of the individual who has died but for the survivors who are left behind.

MYSTERY SOLVED

Past experiences may affect how one responds when a loved one is dying.

When I was in my early forties, I decided to go back to school and get a master's degree in nursing. Getting a master's degree had been on my Bucket List for quite some time. I suddenly realized if I was going to achieve this goal, I had better get it done before my children started college and the opportunity was lost.

I found the coursework fascinating and quickly formed a study group with three other students, which was a great help in processing all the new information I was learning. One of my favorite classes was a research course called Clinical Phenomena. The Grounded Theory Methodology used in Clinical Phenomena was different from the usual research methods where the researcher forms a hypothesis, manipulates variables and analyzes the resulting data. When using Grounded Theory, the researcher starts with a question regarding some phenomenon that has been observed and through a process of questioning arrives at its cause.

I think I was drawn to this research method because I am a big fan of mysteries and this type of research is like solving a crime. One asks questions and puts clues together until one discovers "who done it." Now all I needed to do was identify some clinical mystery I wanted to "solve."

While going to school I was also working part-time for a local hospice, making nursing visits to people who were terminally ill and living at home. The majority of these individuals were being cared for by family members. Most strongly desired to remain at home throughout their illness. When hospice patients reached the final stage of illness, their caregivers were given detailed instructions regarding what changes to expect and how to care for their loved ones. A nurse was available 24/7 to make a home visit if needed. With this kind of support, the majority of families were able to successfully handle a home death.

During the next few days I found myself looking back, mentally reviewing various families I had worked with over the past few months, trying

73

to identify a clinical phenomenon I wanted to explore. I kept drawing a blank. I just couldn't seem to identify anything to research. I was about to discard my whole idea and rethink my project when I received a call from one of the on-call nurses, notifying me that one of my patients, Clyde Saunders, had been admitted to the inpatient unit the night before. The inpatient unit was a special unit in our hospital where hospice patients could be admitted if they needed intense nursing care or if their families were unable to manage their final stage of care at home. The on-call nurse had been contacted by Mary, Clyde's wife, who stated she was no longer able to care for her husband at home and demanded that he be admitted.

I was surprised to hear of Clyde's admission. I had visited the couple the day before and everything seemed fine. Clyde had become weaker over the past several months as his lung cancer advanced, but he was comfortable, and his pain was well controlled. His breathing had become more labored, so I had ordered some oxygen for him to use if he felt he needed it. During our discussion, Clyde talked about how much he hated hospitals and how important it was to him to die at home. Mary had seemed completely on-board with the plan of a home death. What had happened? Was it a lack of support? Had I failed somehow to prepare the couple? What had gone wrong? Suddenly I realized I had found the mystery I wanted to explore. I had the topic for my thesis.

I began my research by making a list of families who had experienced unexplained admissions to the inpatient unit when the patient planned to die at home. I found over the last six months there were nine such deaths among my patients alone. Once I had compiled these statistics, I wrote my research proposal and after receiving permission from the Human Subjects and my Thesis Committees, I began contacting caregivers I wished to interview. All agreed to participate in my study.

Armed with my list of questions and a tape recorder, I began my interviews. Once the interview was completed, I gave the tapes to a secretary I had hired to transcribe them for me. Several weeks later, I found myself sitting in the middle of my den floor pondering participants' responses typed on pieces of paper. Nothing was making any sense. None of my respondents could identify reasons for the unexpected admission of their family member. All of them denied having any unmet needs and felt they had had wonderful support. How could I identify a suspect if I couldn't find any clues? Frustrated, I wanted to take all those useless slips of paper and throw them up in the air like confetti. Maybe I should scrap the whole idea and try something else. Discouraged, I started going over the responses one last time.

Suddenly, a remark made by a woman named Barbara Matthews caught my eye. When talking about her husband's illness Barbara had said, "As soon as I heard John's diagnosis of prostate cancer, I knew how he would die in great deal of agonizing pain." Since her husband John's pain had been well controlled throughout his illness, her comment puzzled me. Where had this idea come from? Intrigued, I contacted Barbara and asked if she would be willing to answer a few more questions.

The next morning as Barbara and I settled down with cups of tea on her patio, I turned to Barbara and remarked, "In our last interview you mentioned as soon as you heard his diagnosis, you felt John would die in a great deal of pain. Can you tell me what made you think that would happen to John?"

Barbara looked thoughtful for a moment and then replied, "Just before John was diagnosed, one of our neighbors died of prostate cancer. His wife came over for coffee one morning and as we were talking, she described how horrible her husband's death had been; how much pain he had suffered. She said he had died in agony."

"So, you thought the same thing was going happen to John?"

"I guess I did," Barbara said, nodding thoughtfully. "When I realized John was getting near the end, I suddenly felt panicky. I was afraid something bad was about to happen to him and I wouldn't be able to help him. I was so frightened. I called the nurse and had him admitted even though he begged me not to do it." Barbara began to cry. "I feel terrible. I should have been able to keep him at home like he wanted. I couldn't even bear to go see him in the hospital. I couldn't bear to see him in pain. I should have been with him when he died, but I just couldn't make myself go there. I couldn't bear to see him suffer."

As we talked, I could sense Barbara's guilt and self-condemnation resolving as she began to understand what had happened, why she had panicked. As this understanding grew, Barbara began to forgive herself for how she had responded. "Now the healing can really begin for her," I thought.

I contacted other individuals in the study, and each had experienced a similar dynamic. Until participating in our interviews, these survivors were not only unaware they had such preconceived ideas about how the death of their love one would occur but were also unaware of how these expectations had affected their behavior.

Mary Saunders, for example, related that she was seven when her father, like Clyde, died of lung cancer. She recalled watching her father suddenly hemorrhaging, coughing up bright red blood while she stood terrified at his bedside. "I guess when you ordered the oxygen, I felt Clyde didn't have much longer to live and suddenly I became so frightened. I thought he would need more care than I could possibly give him. That's when I called the nurse and had him moved."

Barry Dean, another participant whose wife had been comatose for several days prior to her death, reported that when Rose remained unresponsive for several days, he became worried something was terribly wrong. Barry had been a gunner on an airplane during World War II. "I had seen men die during the war. When someone was shot, we worked hard to keep them alive until we reached help. Most of the men died before we landed. There was nothing we could do to save them. I couldn't understand what was taking Rose so long to die. I expected it to go much faster. I thought, 'This isn't normal. Something is wrong.'"

Other participants had similar stories. Several, like Barbara, had formed frightening expectations based on information given to them by family or friends. Some, like Mary, were children when they witnessed the death of a parent or grandparent, frightened by an experience they did not understand. As I discussed the findings of my study with them, these survivors became aware of how their emotional state had affected their ability to manage the death at home. With this new understanding, these survivors were able to forgive their behavior and resolve their guilt they were experiencing for failing to carry out their loved one's last wishes. Now they were free to move on with their lives.

The culprit had been found and the mystery had been solved!!

Afterthoughts

I presented this study the following year at the National Hospice Organization's Conference which is attended by hospice nurses throughout the country. Using the insights gathered in this study, hospice nurses now routinely find out what other deaths caregivers have experienced or been told about during their intake process. Negative expectations a caregiver may have are revealed during these conversations. Knowing this gives nurses an opportunity to correct any misinformation or negative expectations which could affect a caregiver's ability to manage a home death. This has resulted in a significant drop in the number of unexpected inpatient admissions among individuals wanting to die at home. It has also reduced the number of survivors left dealing with feelings of guilt over not carrying out their family member's last wishes.

THE HILLMAN FAMILY

Having Advanced Directives in place eases the stress of making end-of-life decisions.

Vic and I talked for many months prior to our retirement about how and where we wanted to spend the next few years. Throughout my career, I had met many "snowbirds" who were full time RVers, meaning instead of having permanent home, they traveled throughout the country living in either a travel trailer, a fifth-wheel, or a motorhome. I loved hearing their stories and envied their carefree lifestyle. One night I suggested to my husband that we buy a motorhome and hit the road. I was flabbergasted when Vic agreed. We put aside a few belongings that we were not ready to part with and put them in storage. We offered our household furnishings to our girls and to our astonishment we discovered there was very little of our things they wanted. An estate sale was held and everything that did not sell was donated to local charities. We were ready to hit the road.

We traveled in our motorhome for eight years. I loved it. It still is my favorite way to travel. I never had to pack; everything I might need was with me (including the kitchen sink), and I slept each night in my own bed.

When my husband decided he was getting to the age that he could no longer safely drive our RV, we decided to settle down in California close to our oldest daughter and her family. We had often stayed in an RV park near her home and through the years had gotten to know the owner Gordon Hillman and his daughter Nancy. Once the decision to stop traveling was made, we called Nancy to discuss becoming permanent residents of the park, something Nancy had been encouraging us to do. Nancy told us a very special space had just become available and she promised to hold it for us.

When we arrived at the RV park, we found the space Nancy had reserved for us was perfect. It was located in a private area of the park and included a small fenced-in yard. A wooden deck ran along one side of our motorhome, and we were surrounded by towering pines.

The park owners, Gordon Hillman and his wife Grace, lived in a house next door. Nancy, knowing I was a nurse, had introduced me to her parents and occasionally asked me to examine them when she became concerned that one of them might be developing a medical problem. The couple, who were in their eighties, had been high school sweethearts. Gordon had joined the Air Force right out of high school and was a pilot during World War II. When Gordon finished basic training, he and Grace were married. After the war, Gordon started a construction company, building commercial buildings such as shopping centers and apartments throughout California. Although Gordon was no longer in the Air Force, he continued to fly. Through the years, Gordon had owned several planes and used them to fly his family to various vacation destinations.

In the early 1980s the couple bought a large parcel of property in the countryside south of San Jose which contained an old winery and several small houses. The family referred to this place as "the ranch" and spent many of their summers there. After their children were grown, Gordon decided to turn the ranch into an RV park. The family had often traveled in an RV and Gordon knew how difficult it was to find nice places to stay. It took several years and much persuasion to get his plans approved by the county, but finally the RV park was constructed. It was beautiful, set against the coastal hills with a year-round stream running through it.

As Gordon and Grace grew older, they decided to live on the property next door to their daughter Nancy, who was managing the park for them. Nancy, who was very close to her parents, checked on them several times a day. She also cooked their meals and took the couple to their doctor appointments.

The Hillmans had raised seven children and at first glance Grace appeared to have been the classical stay-at-home mom. But she too had learned to fly and had won several racing events for woman pilots. Gordon beamed with pride when he talked about her accomplishments.

Raising seven children had taught Grace ways to be a disciplinarian, a skill she still used. Her children, who were now adults, frequently quarreled during family get-togethers when old sibling rivalries reappeared. When these squabbles broke out, Grace had only to say the offenders' names and give them "the look" to quickly restore peace. Along with her ability to be stern, Grace also had a wonderful sense of humor. I asked her during one of my visits if she ever became nervous when flying with Gordon. She looked at me with a mischievous twinkle and replied, "His flying never made me nervous, but his driving sure does." Everyone loved this funny, spunky lady.

I was lying in bed one morning, reading while sipping my first cup of coffee, when there was a sudden loud series of frantic knocks on the RV door. Vic hurried to the door and found Sonny, one of the maintenance crew, standing there looking very upset. "Mr. Hillman wants your wife to come right away," Sonny said. "Mrs. Hillman is very sick and he's worried."

I knew Nancy was away visiting her daughter and grandchildren in Minnesota. If Gordon was asking for help, something must be seriously wrong. Sonny continued to pace anxiously back and forth on our patio while I hurriedly threw on some clothes, grabbed my blood pressure kit and dashed next door.

When I walked into the Hellman's living room, I was shocked to find Grace lying unconscious on the floor with Gordon frantically doing chest compressions. He had a phone cradled between his ear and shoulder and was obviously talking to the 911 operator. "Still giving chest compressions," he said, looking up as I entered.

I tossed my blood pressure kit into the nearest chair and knelt on the floor beside Grace, across from Gordon. "Would you like me to take over?" I asked. Gordon nodded wordlessly and, looking relieved, moved away from his wife. Grace, who was very pale and not breathing, had no discernible pulse. As I continued doing chest compressions, her skin seemed to grow a little pinker, but I could not feel a pulse despite my efforts to revive her.

I knew the paramedics were on the way, but it would take the ambulance ten or fifteen minutes to arrive. While I continued doing compressions, Gordon called his oldest daughter, Bertha, to let her know what had happened. Finally, we heard the sound of a siren in the distance and soon the paramedics walked through the door, closely followed by Bertha. It was with a huge sense of relief that I moved away from Grace and let the paramedics take over.

Bertha looked around angrily, demanding to know what had happened to her mother. I explained that Grace had suddenly collapsed and quit breathing. Frightened, Gordon had dialed 911 and then sent Sonny to get me so I could help until the paramedics arrived.

While Bertha and I stood talking, the paramedics were continuing the chest compressions, while gently lifting Grace unto a stretcher and into the waiting ambulance. With sirens blaring, they drove away. Without another word, Bertha gathered up her father and left for the hospital where Grace was being taken. Quietly, I retrieved my blood pressure kit, turned out the lights and closed the door. As I walked back home, I was filled with a sudden sadness, knowing I had probably seen Grace for the last time.

I didn't hear any more about Grace until the following morning when I got a call from Nancy. She had flown back from Minnesota as soon as she heard the news about her mother. Once back home, she had gone directly from the airport to the hospital. She had arrived just as the doctors were meeting with Grace's family. A tumor in Grace's throat had blocked her airway causing Grace's collapse. Grace was now on a ventilator in the Intensive Care unit. The doctor told the family that the tumor had prevented Grace from getting sufficient oxygen after her collapse and he feared extensive brain damage may have occurred despite my efforts and those of the paramedics.

According to Nancy, the doctor told the family that if their mother had not received CPR she would have died before reaching the hospital. Nancy said, "My family asked me to thank you for saving Mom's life.

We are so grateful you were there to help her." While I knew CPR had played its part, I felt the real reason Grace was still alive was her determination to give her family a chance to say their goodbyes. When I repeated this thought to Nancy, I could tell she didn't really understand what I was saying.

That evening, a very upset Nancy stopped by to give me an update. Tests the doctor had ordered showed that due to the lack of oxygen, Grace did indeed have extensive brain damage. Her brain was essentially dead, not able to send out the signals needed for Grace to breathe on her own. Only the ventilator was keeping her alive. The doctor recommended that the family consider stopping this life support, as Grace's situation was hopeless.

As the family slowly absorbed this news and its implications a heated debate began. Gordon was not ready to let his wife die. He continued to hold out hope for Grace's recovery, saying, "There could be a miracle. No one really knows what God has in mind. We'll just bring Mom home on the ventilator, hire nurses to take care of her, and wait and see what God has in mind." Several of his children were in agreement with this plan.

Gary, the oldest, was the practical dollars-and-sense one in the family. "Dad be reasonable," he protested. "There is no way you could afford something like that. The insurance won't cover that kind of care and it is too expensive for you to pay for it yourself. Besides, what good is it going to do? Mom is basically gone. Even if she did somehow regain consciousness, the doctors say the tumor is probably cancer and would eventually kill her. Maybe this is a blessing in disguise. Think of how she would suffer if she lived." Several of the siblings agreed with him, feeling that efforts to keep their mother alive were futile. The lines were drawn regarding Grace's care and the family appeared deadlocked. Because of their emotional stress, it was difficult for family members to think rationally, and without Grace's calming influence, tempers flared.

Grace had no Living Will, a document that provides guidance to families in this type of situation. Would Grace want to be kept on life support? No one knew. Like many families, they had never discussed these issues. By law, Gordon, as her husband, had the final say regarding Grace's medical care and whether life support would be continued.

Realizing the family's distress, the doctor wisely gave them three days to come up with a decision. The family's first two options were for Grace to either be discharged on the ventilator to a nursing home or to her own home with nursing supervision. The third was to take Grace off the ventilator and discontinue further efforts to keep her artificially alive. The decision was up to the family.

To help the family make their decision, the doctor suggested they gather more information by talking to their minister, the hospital social worker, and a palliative care team physician, something the family reluctantly agreed to do.

When Nancy stopped by several nights later, she announced, "We have decided to take Mom off life support tomorrow. We all agree that Mom would not have any kind of life if we try to keep her alive on machines. She would hate that. Dad finally realized that Mom has already left us. It's not fair to her to keep prolonging things just because it's hard for us to let her go."

"I think the only reason your mom is still here is because she wanted to give all of you a chance to say goodbye," I repeated once again. "You are probably right," Nancy agreed. "That sounds just like her."

The next morning, Grace was moved into a private room. Her teary family gathered at her bedside. The family's minister arrived just as Grace was being given medication to ensure she felt no discomfort. The ventilator was removed, and the room was quiet except for the prayers being murmured by the family. Without the ventilator, Grace's chest became still, not moving as the machine no longer pushed air in and out of her lungs. She looked as though she were in a deep sleep. Her heart beat its last few beats, and she was gone. Quietly each family member said their own personal goodbye to Grace and together they left the hospital room.

At the funeral held several days later, I found myself being introduced to various friends and family members. During each introduction, I heard my name said, followed by, "This is the lady who gave us a chance to tell Mom goodbye." I knew that my message to Grace's family had finally been understood.

ADVANCE DIRECTIVES

Why are Advanced Directives so important?

My experience with the Hillmans is a good example of what can happen if someone is dying and unable to make decisions about their end-of-life care and they have no Advance Directives in place. A Living Will and a Medical Power of Attorney (MPOA) can prevent some of the stress our families may feel if they are required to make end-of-life decisions without knowing what we would like them to do. A living will, states what treatment one does and does not want should we have an irreversible condition and can't make those decisions for ourselves. Would we want a feeding tube to prolong life if we have end-stage Alzheimer's disease or a tumor in our throat like Grace and are unable to eat? Would we want to continue living if we had to spend our life in a coma or on a ventilator? If we died, do we want CPR used to try to bring us back to life? Having a living will ensures we make these decisions for ourselves and not burden our family with making them for us.

Sometimes people have the mistaken belief that if they suddenly became seriously ill or injured, they will not receive treatment if there is a living will in place. Quite the opposite is true. If a person develops a serious medical condition like a heart attack or stroke, is injured in an accident or is found unconscious, his condition will be treated, and tests will be performed to find out what is causing the person's symptoms. It is only when the physician has determined the condition is irreversible and there is no more that can be done to save the individual, that the directions in the living will are followed.

During my years in hospice, one of my jobs was to discuss terminating life support with families like the Hillmans. Whenever I worked with families in this type of situation, I asked the decision-makers to consider several things. First, I reminded the family that it is the person's medical condition that is causing the death of their loved one, not the termination of life support or treatment. I pointed out that in all probability the death would have already occurred if well-intended medical interventions hadn't been implemented.

When there is no appointed decision-maker and no living will exist, family members, like the Hillmans, often find themselves arguing about the type of care their loved one should receive. These disagreements may go on for several days, often creating bitter feelings which may last for years. A living will, prevents this type of scenario from happening. In addition to having a living will, it is recommended that you also designate someone you trust to be your Medical Power of Attorney (MPOA). This is a person you authorize to make medical decisions for you if you are not able to do so for yourself. The living will together with a Medical Power of Attorney are called Advance Directives. In many states, when an individual is unable to make treatment decisions and there is no MPOA, the power to give consent for treatment goes to the person's spouse. If there is no living spouse or the spouse is unable to make those decisions, the decision-making responsibility rests on the children's shoulders. If there are no children, it is up to the next closest blood relative such as the dying person's siblings to direct the individual's end-of-life care. An Ethics Committee, made up of people selected by the hospital, may have the power to remove life support or stop curative treatments if the dying individual has no living relatives. But these laws vary. Texas, for example, gives the doctor the right to terminate life support if the patient is "brain dead" even if the family wants to continue supportive measures. It is important to become familiar with the laws in your state.

If you are someone's MPOA, it is important to discuss the person's wishes with them and clarify any questions you may have. For example, my father's living will stated he did not want to be placed on a ventilator. However, he had emphysema and had experienced frequent bouts of pneumonia. At some point, I knew he might need to be placed on a ventilator temporarily until he was once again able to breathe on his own. As his MPOA, I needed more information. When asked what he would like me to do in this situation, my dad replied, "I'll leave that decision up to you. If you think it is necessary for me to be on a ventilator and that it is temporary, fine. But if I can't breathe without the ventilator, you better see that it is stopped. If you leave me stuck living on that thing, I'll come back and haunt you." Well, I certainly had a clear understanding of what my dad's wishes were after that conversation! This discussion with my dad not only clarified his wishes but also made me realize how important it is to choose an MPOA you can trust to carry out your wishes. I was very grateful my parents took responsibility for seeing their directives were in place long before they were needed. It made my job so much easier because I had a clear understanding of what their wishes were.

People may turn to their physician for guidance when a family member is seriously ill, thinking, "The doctor knows more about all this than I do. I am going to let him make the decisions." This may or may not be a good strategy. Physicians, by training, are healers. If a patient is experiencing symptoms, medical doctors are trained to determine what causes the symptoms and ways to treat the disease or injury. To do this, physicians often follow medical algorithms or decision trees. Decision trees list symptoms that maybe occurring, such as chest pain, followed by a list of tests to be ordered to determine the cause of the pain. Depending on what the tests results show, the person's condition is diagnosed, and a variety of treatment options are listed. From these options, the physician chooses the one he feels is optimal for that individual. For many doctors, this type of decision-making becomes automatic.

Decision trees are useful and a wonderful way to train medical practitioners. Unfortunately, many doctors do not pause to assess what else is going on with the person. Does he have a chronic or terminal disease? What is the quality of the life she is living right now? Will treatment make his ability to enjoy life better or worse? What is the patient's or his family's wishes?

In recent years many medical schools have begun addressing this situation, teaching their students to recognize when further treatment is futile and how to discuss discontinuing curative treatment or life support with patients and families, something which is understandably difficult to do. However, there are still many doctors who continue to order just one more test, treatment or surgery regardless of the patient's condition.

Patty, a writing friend of mine, had an experience with one such physician. Patty and her husband Carl were very involved with Carl's aging parents. Lois, Carl's mother, was in the advanced stages of Alzheimer's disease and the couple were overseeing her care. Early one morning, Patty received a phone call from the adult care home where Lois was living, informing Patty that Lois had fallen and was complaining of hip pain. The EMT's had been called and were about to transport Lois to the local hospital for evaluation. Patty, already rummaging for her car keys, said she would meet them at the hospital as soon as possible.

When Patty arrived at the Emergency Department, she learned that Lois's X-rays revealed her mother-in-law had broken her hip. Soon an orthopedic surgeon arrived, introduced himself to Patty and announced that he was taking Lois to surgery for a hip replacement. Patty, who describes herself as someone who is usually a people-pleaser, doesn't like making waves kind of person, looked the surgeon in the eye and said, "No, no you're not. No surgery." The doctor looked at Patty in disbelief. "Don't you understand? Her hip is broken; we have to fix it," he snapped, looking outraged.

"She has advanced Alzheimer's disease," Patty explained. "She doesn't know what is going on. If you operate, she won't understand what is happening. She'll be absolutely terrified, and I refuse to put her through that. I just want to keep her comfortable. She just needs something, so she won't be in pain."

"We have to operate," the surgeon insisted, becoming increasingly irritated at what he viewed as an unreasonable relative who didn't know what she was talking about.

"I am her Medical Power of Attorney along with my husband," Patty replied. "You need my permission to operate and I am not giving it. No surgery."

The doctor huffed off and Patty thought the matter had been settled. Soon the surgeon returned, followed by three other orthopedic surgeons, each demanding that Patty allow them to operate. One became so outraged at her refusal, he said, "Don't you know she will die if we don't operate? You understand, that don't you? You are killing her."

Patty stood her ground, refusing to give consent for the surgery. Since Lois was not competent to give consent because of her Alzheimer's, the surgeons had no choice but to walk away.

After their departure, Patty asked to speak to someone on the Palliative Care team. She knew that Palliative Care was designed to work with individuals with terminal illnesses, managing their symptoms and providing support to families. When the Palliative Care doctor arrived and heard Patty's story, he was appalled. "You did exactly the right thing," he reassured Patty. It would be cruel to put your mother-in-law through the trauma of surgery. It also would be pointless, because at this stage of her illness, she probably won't be able to walk again regardless of what is done."

Those orthopedic surgeons who spoke to Patty were obviously using the decision tree they had been trained to follow. Broken hip = Is the patient physically strong enough for surgery? If yes = perform hip replacement. Sadly, there is no place in this decision tree that asks: What other medical conditions does the patient have? Will the patient be able to participate in physical therapy? What are the family's wishes? Since most broken hips occur in the elderly, shouldn't these questions be added to the doctor's decision-making process? Luckily for Lois, she had an MPOA with the legal authority to stop the surgeon from operating.

After completing his evaluation, the Palliative Care physician arranged for Lois to be moved to a skilled nursing facility and admitted to hospice.

He also ordered pain medication to treat Lois's discomfort. Lois died peacefully in her sleep several weeks later.

Sometimes, a doctor will continue ordering tests and treatments because the physician isn't comfortable talking to family members about stopping curative treatment. I suspect this is what happened in the case of Don.

Jeanette, a good friend of mine, dropped by one morning to talk about her ex-husband Don, who was currently in Intensive Care at a nearby hospital. Although Don was only in his late fifties, he had multiple health issues. He suffered from severe depression which only increased in his early thirties when he was diagnosed with multiple sclerosis. When he developed diabetes along with the MS, Don became angry at the world, feeling it was unfair that he should have to suffer with these multiple health issues. No longer able to work, Don sat at home and watched TV while snacking on potato chips and eating fast food. He frequently refused to inject his insulin, causing his blood sugar to rise to dangerous levels, resulting in numerous complications such as the loss of vision in one eye and the amputation of his left leg. Eventually, Don developed dementia caused by his MS. Don, when rational, often stated he wished he could just die and get it over with. In a way, his continual refusal to follow the prescribed medical regimen was a form of slow, gradual suicide.

A severe pneumonia caused Don's latest hospitalization and his infection was not responding to antibiotics. During the two weeks he had been in the hospital, Don's doctors treated his pneumonia with one medication after another without much success. Now Don's kidneys were beginning to fail and his physicians wanted to start dialysis.

Unfortunately, Don had no Advance Directives. His only two relatives were his son Adam and his daughter Ashley, who were both in their early twenties. Since Don's doctors felt he was incompetent to make his own decisions regarding his medical treatment, it was up to his two children to make those decisions for him. Jeanette had been visiting Don along with her children, and she was concerned about the emotional toll the situation was having on them. Ashley and Adam were feeling that further treatment was pointless but did not know what to do or how to make the doctors stop. Jeanette asked if I would talk to them about hospice.

We met that evening in the waiting room of the ICU, where I listened to Adam and Ashley express their distress about their father's situation. "The doctors keep wanting to try one more thing," Ashley said, beginning to cry. "Nothing they are doing is helping him. Dad is miserable and I can't stand seeing him suffer like this." Adam nodded in agreement.

We discussed hospice and the idea of stopping curative treatment and switching to palliative care which would focus on keeping Don comfortable. The two liked that idea; it seemed more in line with what they felt was best for their father and what they knew he would want. The pair decided to discuss contacting hospice with Don's doctor the following morning.

Jeanette called the next day, sounding pleased. Adam and Ashley had mentioned hospice to Don's physician, who much to their surprise readily agreed, saying, "I think hospice is a very good idea."

Don was admitted to hospice that afternoon and was moved to their inpatient unit. Here, unlike the ICU, visiting hours were unrestricted and Don's children could see their father whenever and as often as they wished. After Don's transfer, the hospice bereavement counselor began meeting with Adam and Ashley. With the counselor's help, the siblings were able to begin expressing their grief at losing their father and their anger at his refusal to take better care of himself. Don died several weeks later.

Most family members find the decision to stop treatment or life support a difficult one to make, especially if the terminally ill individual is a child or younger adult. It is also very hard to make these decisions when the family has no idea what their loved one would want them to do.

I feel strongly that medical staff should not pressure families or try to influence their decisions. Instead, families should be given the information they need and left to decide for themselves whether to continue treatment or life support or opt for palliative care. Health-care workers, like those orthopedic surgeons, may think they know what is best for the patient but family members who know the person's situation may not share their feelings. Keep in mind, it's the family who must live with the consequences of these decisions.

Experience has taught me that one of the kindest things one can do for our own families is to put the proper paperwork in place and discuss your own personal wishes with your family and your MPOA. With this type of preparation, our family members will have the information needed to make the decisions they feel you would want them to make. Knowing your wishes helps prevent family members from feeling guilty about terminating life-prolonging measures and allows them to take satisfaction in knowing your wishes have been carried out.

MR. BALDWIN

Respecting other people's choices can be challenging.

"Good luck with this one," Marlene said, handing me a hospice referral. "It sounds like a real challenge." I read through the form which stated Mrs. Mary Baldwin had called the hospice office requesting a nursing visit. She was worried about her husband Tom. According to the information she had provided, she suspected her husband had cancer and was in a great deal of pain, but he was refusing to see a doctor. Sensing Mary was under a great deal of stress, I called the Baldwin home and made an appointment to see the couple that afternoon.

When I arrived at the Baldwins' house, I knew I was about to encounter a difficult situation, one that would require a great deal of patience, understanding and sensitivity. I hoped I was up to the challenge. Mary Baldwin opened the door and gave me a welcoming smile. She was a small, motherly woman in her late seventies who looked exhausted. Mary greeted me, saying, "I am so glad to see you. Tom is in so much pain. He has been sick for weeks now and his pain just keeps getting worse. I can't stand seeing him like this. He's not eating or sleeping, and he won't see a doctor. I just don't know what to do or where to turn for help. My neighbor told me about hospice, and I decided to call and see if there was anything you could possibly do to help us. Come, I'll introduce you to Tom."

As we started walking toward the living room, Mary began looking a little nervous. "I told Tom you were coming," she said, "but he isn't very happy about talking to you. Tom doesn't think much of people in the medical profession, so I'm not sure what kind of a reception you are going to get. I'm hoping he will be cooperative."

I followed Mary into the living room, where we found Tom sitting in a recliner, his right leg propped up on several pillows, watching the news on TV. As Mary introduce me, Mr. Baldwin turned and glowered at me, not acknowledging the introduction. He sat, his body rigid, arms folded across his chest, looking like a hostile witness who had just been asked to testify against his best friend. I sat down in a nearby chair, saying "I understand you aren't very happy about seeing me today, Mr. Baldwin. I came because your wife is very worried about you. She tells me you have been having a lot of pain. Seeing you in such terrible pain is very difficult for her. Your neighbor thought maybe hospice could offer your wife some help and support, help her understand what is happening to you. That's why I am here. Would you mind telling me what's been going on? Where you are having the pain?"

"This is what's going on," said Mr. Baldwin angrily as he turned to expose the back of his right leg. I stifled a gasp as I saw the cause of his distress. There was the largest melanoma (a mole that had become cancerous) I had ever seen. It was an ugly, grapefruit-sized, black lump protruding from the back of Mr. Baldwin's lower leg. The area surrounding the tumor was swollen and red and I guessed the growth had metastasized to other parts of his body as well. "No wonder this poor man is in such terrible pain," I thought. "He must find walking sheer torture."

"Wow," I said taking a deep breath. "That's really something. I can understand why your leg is so painful. Are you having pain anywhere else?" "I have some other pains here and there," Mr. Baldwin replied, continuing to glare at me, "but my leg is the worse. Don't get any ideas about giving me any of that dope you folks like to give out," he added. "I don't believe in taking that stuff. I have my own way of handling things. I don't need any interference from you." He continued to sit, arms folded, daring me to convince him otherwise.

"Mr. Baldwin, I respect your right to handle this situation any way you wish," I said. "How you choose to deal with your pain is entirely up to you. I have no right to tell you what to do. I am curious, though, about what you are doing to help with the pain. Can you tell me about that?"

Mr. Baldwin continued to eye me suspiciously as he explained he was a member of a religion which did not believe in medical intervention. According to his beliefs, one's healing came through God, not doctors. He had been raised in this religion and his faith was the center of his life.

Mr. Baldwin had attended the same church for over fifty years and was one of its founding members. The church had no priests or ministers; instead pastoral responsibilities were performed by members of the congregation who were elected to various positions in the church's hierarchy. Mr. Baldwin had held many of these positions during his fifty years of church attendance. Presently, his duties included overseeing the regular Sunday services plus arranging healing groups whenever a church member fell ill and needed help. In addition, he offered religious guidance to members who requested his help. The church's healing practices had served Mr. Baldwin well. The only time in his 78 years Mr. Baldwin had seen a doctor, he told me proudly, was when he needed to get a blood test for his marriage license.

When Mr. Baldwin noticed a mole growing on the back of his leg, he remembered the cancer warning signs he had heard over the years and suspected the mole was malignant. He immediately set about curing his condition. A healing group was formed, and meetings were held several times a week. Individuals offered prayers and Mr. Baldwin focused his attention on affirmations which reinforced the belief that one could be healed by God. But despite it all, the mole had continued to grow. When the cancer was not healed, Mr. Baldwin was filled with a sense of shame. This devout man believed he had failed both God and the members of his church by his inability to cure his melanoma. "After all, we know God's not at fault," he said. "I am the guilty one. I wavered in my belief. I blocked His healing by losing my faith and allowing fear and doubt to enter my thinking." Mr. Baldwin bowed his head when he said these words and blinked back tears.

My heart went out to this poor man whose physical pain paled beside the emotional and spiritual pain he was experiencing. "I wish I knew a way to ease his suffering," I thought. I also wondered if Mr. Baldwin believed the pain, he was experiencing was punishment for what he perceived as his failure of faith.

I knew if I was to have any chance of working with Mr. Baldwin, I would have to approach him slowly and gently or he would become angry and slam the door in my face. The poor man looked exhausted by the end of my visit. I told him how much I appreciated meeting him, thanked him for helping me understand his beliefs and for allowing me to visit. I mentally crossed my fingers when I asked if I could come visit again, adding I felt Mary needed emotional support. Much to my relief, he agreed to let me return and I set up a time to visit the following week.

Mr. Baldwin's refusal to see a physician complicated his situation. In order to admit Mr. Baldwin officially into the hospice program, it was necessary for a doctor, to sign a form stating Mr. Baldwin was terminally ill. Visiting a physician was something I knew Mr. Baldwin would not agree to do. I decided to discuss the situation with Dr. Long, the hospice Medical Director, and ask his advice.

My opportunity to talk to Dr. Long came several days later during our weekly hospice team meeting. Dr. Long agreed that I should continue seeing Mr. Baldwin despite the fact he couldn't officially become a hospice patient. The team felt the couple badly needed our help.

Over the following weeks, I gradually began to gain Mr. Baldwin's trust. I knew we had forged a bond the day he asked me to call him Mr. B, the nickname used by many of his friends.

Pain control was the biggest problem. I knew better than to bring up the subject of medication, but Mr. B was willing to try icing his tumor, a "non-medical treatment" which provided some relief. As he became weaker, Mary and I came up with ways to make things easier for him: a commode so he wouldn't have to walk to the bathroom, a chair so he could sit down to shower, and Ensure to boost his calories. A wheelchair, obtained from the community loan chest, made it possible for Mr. B to sit in his garden and watch the birds, something he loved to do.

Arizona, like most states, has a law which states that if there is no physician to sign the death certificate when someone dies, that individual must be autopsied by the coroner. Since Mr. B had no physician, the coroner would have to autopsy him. I knew Mr. B would be horrified by the idea of being autopsied and needed to know about this law. But I hated having to bring up the subject. I knew he would be upset.

The next day, when Mr. B and I were seated comfortably in his garden, I began the conversation I had been dreading. "I don't know if you are aware of this, Mr. B, I said cautiously, giving him a concerned look, "but there is a state law which says when a death occurs a doctor must sign a death certificate stating what caused the person's death. If no doctor with this information is available, an autopsy must be performed by the coroner to determine the cause of death. No burial or cremation can take place until the autopsy is completed. According to this law, when you die an autopsy will have to be performed unless we do something now to prevent that from happening."

Looking shocked, Mr. B said, "That's what happens? In every case? Why?" "The authorities need to find out why the person died, to make sure the person died from natural causes and the death wasn't a homicide or suicide," I explained. "If the person has no doctor, there is no one who can give the authorities this information."

There was a long pause while Mr. Baldwin processed this information. "You couldn't just tell them I had cancer?" he finally asked. "I wish I could," I said. "That would make things so much easier, but unfortunately it has to be a doctor that determines the cause of death and who signs the death certificate. Because of this law, your choices are either to see a physician so he or she knows about your condition or to be autopsied later. I'm sorry. I know this isn't something you wanted to hear. I'll give you some time to think about what you want to do." I left a stunned Mr. Baldwin pondering this unwelcome news. For a man who had spent his entire life avoiding physicians, he was facing what felt like an impossible choice.

Mary called me early the next morning. "Tom is wondering if you could stop by sometime today," she said. "He's been quite upset since your visit yesterday and wants to talk to you as soon as possible." We set a time for me to stop by later that afternoon. When I arrived, I had barely taken my customary seat when Mr. B looked at me and said, "I was awake all night thinking about what you said. An autopsy would be awfully hard on Mary and I can't stand the idea of being cut open. How do we stop it?"

"Why don't you let our hospice director, Dr. Long, examine you?" I suggested. "He would only have to see you once. He'll just ask you a few questions and check you over. Once he's examined you, you won't ever have to see him again. When the time comes, he can sign the certificate for you. If you want, I would be glad to make an appointment for you," I added.

"Let me think about it," Mr. B said. Because of his distrust of the medical profession, including me, Mr. Baldwin called a friend who was an attorney and verified that the information I had given him was indeed correct. Satisfied, Mr. B reluctantly agreed to see Dr. Long.

The day after the doctor's visit, I stopped by to find out how things had gone. "I was so frightened," Mr. B confessed. "The doctor was running late and by the time I finally saw him, I was shaking all over. He was very nice, and he didn't try to push a bunch of medicine at me. But I'm so glad that's over," Mr. Baldwin added, shaking his head. "I never want to go through that again."

When I talked to Dr. Long, he confirmed that Mr. Baldwin did indeed have a melanoma. "I've never seen anything like it," the doctor said. "I suggested he have a little radiation to reduce the size of the tumor and relieve some of his pain, but he refused, and I didn't push it. He also refused pain medication, but I will be happy to prescribe something if he changes his mind."

Now that Mr. Baldwin had seen a doctor, we were finally able to admit him to the hospice program. With Mr. B's consent, I arranged for one of our aides to visit several times a week to help him bathe, which took some of the caregiving load off Mary's shoulders. A social worker met with the couple and helped them complete funeral arrangements.

As Mr. B's disease progressed and death grew nearer, his spiritual pain seemed to increase. Because of his feelings of guilt and shame, Mr. B was facing death without the spiritual comfort he ordinarily would receive from his church. Although church members had continued praying for him, Mr. B had cut off all communication with his congregation, refusing to see visitors or to accept phone calls. One day when Mr. B seemed unusually agitated, I suggested he let Mark, our hospice chaplain come pray with him. I was delighted when he agreed to allow Mark to visit. Mark's special skill was helping individuals resolve the many complex spiritual issues that can occur at the end of someone's life, something Mr. Baldwin badly needed. The two men hit it off immediately. Soon Mark was making regular visits to the Baldwin household. The men had great discussions about their varying religious beliefs, discussions they both enjoyed. Gradually, Mr. B came to trust Mark and to respect his opinions.

With Mark's help, Mr. Baldwin began to view his situation differently. Through their discussions, Mr. B came to believe his unsuccessful attempt to heal his tumor was not a spiritual failure; rather it was an indication that his time on earth was up and God was simply calling him home. His work was done.

Once he was spiritually at peace, Mr. B began to allow visits from church members wanting to say their goodbyes and to offer him their love and support. Toward the end, Mary had to limit the number of visitors to prevent Tom from becoming overly tired. With the urging of both Mary and his congregation, Mr. B. finally agreed to take medication to control his pain.

Mr. B died peacefully several months later, surrounded by his wife, children and several church members who were especially close to him. As I sat at Mr. B's funeral listening to members of his congregation honoring this remarkable man, I found myself feeling very grateful he had come into my life. He had taught me so much about how important it is to respect the way each individual chooses to experience their dying process and how to find ways to facilitate their choices. I was also very grateful we had found a way to avoid an autopsy.

Afterthoughts

Mr. B's feelings of guilt and shame at his failure to cure himself are not unusual. When there is no medical cure for an illness, individuals may seek alternative medicine to heal their diseases, often turning to books which describe self-healing methods through the use of herbs, diets, prayer, meditation, visualizations or positive thinking. For this group, belief in the curative power of an alternative therapy helps restore a sense of empowerment and control which had long been absent in the person's life. However, if the disease continues unabated despite their efforts, their sense of empowerment may be replaced by a sense of failure over not producing the hoped-for cure.

One of my patients called this the "Burden of New Age Thinking." She described it this way: "When you hear or read about people who have healed themselves, you begin to believe you too have the power to cure your illness if only you have enough belief in that power, pray hard enough, eat the right things, take the necessary herbs or think the right thoughts. When your cancer doesn't go away, you are consumed by feelings of shame and guilt. You feel you have failed not only yourself but also your family, who must now assume the burden of caring for you. You start wondering, 'What is wrong with me? Why can't I do this healing thing?' Anger and depression are not far behind."

Ruth, a hospice patient I visited, had a slightly more realistic approach. She had been through a variety of medical treatments – chemotherapy, surgery, radiation – which had failed to stop the growth of her cancer. Since Western medicine was unable to stop her disease, Ruth decided to try a diet which proponents claimed cured her type of cancer. The diet was very complicated and the foods it recommended took a great deal of time and effort to prepare. When Ruth discussed the diet with me, she said, "If it doesn't work, at least I will know I tried everything I could to get rid of the cancer. And even if it doesn't help," Ruth add with a grin, "this diet keeps me so busy cooking I don't have time to worry about myself."

Sometimes diseases do respond to alternative medical practices. Occasionally miraculous healings, or as we in the medical field like to call them, "spontaneous remissions", do occur for reasons that cannot be medically explained. But all too often alternative therapies are ineffective.

To help people dispel their sense of failure when these remedies don't produce the desired results, I remind these individuals that they don't experience a sense of personal failure when traditional medical practices such as chemotherapy, radiation or surgery fail to cure their disease. Instead, they blame the therapy for not doing the job: the "chemo failed to kill the cancer" mentality. When health-care providers become aware that feelings like guilt and shame are occurring, they can work with these individuals and help dispel their sense of personal failure.

JIM AND CAROL BROWN

Our emotional state often controls the decisions we make when someone we love is dying.

Carol Brown and I became friends in grade school. We were inseparable throughout high school and were college roommates. After college, we each married and moved to different parts of the country but somehow, we managed to stay in touch. When Carol was in her late thirties, her husband, Steve, died, leaving her with three children to raise on her own. Although, Steve had some insurance, the policy did not provide enough money to pay the monthly bills. Fortunately, Carol, who until now had been a stay-at-home mom, found a job teaching fourth grade at a nearby school. During the next few years, Carol made teaching and her children the center of her life. When her youngest went off to college, friends wondered what Carol was going to do with her life now that her children were grown.

Carol met Jim Brown one night at a church bingo party. Jim, whose wife had recently died, found Carol a sympathetic listener. The two began to look forward to their weekly meetings at bingo and often went out for coffee afterwards. As the months passed, Carol found herself growing fond of Jim but was reluctant to let him become anything more than just a friend. Carol had been devastated by Steve's death and she had vowed she would never go through that kind of emotional pain again.

It took Jim several years to overcome Carol's resistance and convince her to marry him. When Carol called to tell me she had finally said yes, she threatened to demand Jim get a physical before she agreed to say, "I do." Although we laughed at her joke, I knew deep down Carol was frightened at the thought of being vulnerable once again.

Carol had always wanted to live near the ocean, so Jim found a job working at a nuclear plant located in a small town along the California Central Coast. Carol loved living there. The two settled into married life and started making friends. Often when the weather was warm enough, the pair would walk to the beach and watch the sunset while they ate the picnic dinner Carol had prepared. They were delighted when Carol's kids and grandchildren became frequent visitors. Carol's children soon grew to love Jim and began calling him Pops, making him feel a real part of their family. The next few years were happy ones for all of them.

This newfound happiness was suddenly shattered one day six years later, when Carol received a phone call from Jim's supervisor. Jim had begun suffering chest pains at work. The paramedics had been called and had they taken Jim to the local hospital. A neighbor drove a very shaky Carol to the Emergency Department, where she was told Jim had suffered a massive heart attack. If he survived, Jim would need open heart surgery as soon his condition was stable. Carol was terrified. How could this be happening again? She doubted she had the courage to face losing another husband.

Laura, Carol's daughter, lived in Los Angles. When Laura learned about her stepfather's heart attack, she dropped everything and drove straight to the hospital to be with her mother. It was several days before the pair received the news that Jim would survive. A week later, he was strong enough for surgery and his doctors performed a quadruple by-pass.

Laura called me several days later. Carol was too overwhelmed by her anxiety and fear to make calls herself and had asked Laura to let me know what had happened. Laura promised to keep me updated on Jim's condition.

The next few weeks were a nightmare for Carol. Seeing her husband lying in ICU connected to tubes and monitors brought back terrible memories. Carol had to force herself to visit Jim and was badly shaken each time she saw him. Fortunately, Jim's surgery went smoothly and two weeks later he was finally strong enough to come home. Although Jim had made it through his heart attack and subsequent surgery, his heart had been severely damaged. Jim found he tired easily and was no longer able to work. Without Jim's income, the couple were forced to sell their home and move into a mobile home park located in a small town several hundred miles away.

During his hospitalization, the doctors discovered in addition to his heart disease, Jim also had developed diabetes. He was put on a special diet and told he needed to exercise. His doctor encouraged Jim to start going for daily walks. Since Jim loved to eat and hated walking, he refused to do either, much to the dismay of Carol and his new cardiologist. Carol's attempts to see that Jim ate only the foods listed on his diet were constantly defeated by Jim's trips to the grocery store where he purchased the cookies, candy and potato chips he considered an essential part of his diet. After several months of arguing and pleading, Carol finally gave up trying to get Jim to follow his doctor's orders. She knew she had to accept the fact that Jim would do what he wanted, regardless of the consequences to his health.

Once Jim was feeling better, the couple began to settle into their new lives. Soon Jim was running the mobile home park's weekly bingo games and Carol joined the woman's club. Since Jim was no longer working, he helped Carol with the household chores, fixing the couple's breakfast each morning, doing some of the cleaning and cooking dinner several times a week. Carol fears began to recede as their lives returned to a new kind of normal.

Soon after Carol and Jim moved to the mobile home park, my husband and I quit RVing and settled down in California, near our oldest daughter. Since we now lived only 270 miles from the Browns, we visited the couple several times a year. After our many years apart, I enjoyed being able to be spend time with Carol once again. It was also nice to have an opportunity to get to know Jim and to reconnect with Carol's two girls, who would sometimes join us for the weekend.

About five years later, Jim began experiencing severe leg cramps whenever he walked. Tests revealed the arteries in his legs had become clogged. Surgery to repair the damaged arteries needed to be done and a date was set for the operation. During Jim's preoperative exam, a huge bulging in the large blood vessel in Jim's abdomen was discovered. It was an aortic aneurysm and needed to be repaired immediately before it ruptured. Suddenly, Jim was facing not one but two surgeries.

The next few weeks were anxious ones, filled with doctors' appointments, surgeries and hospital stays. Laura once again found herself making the two-hour drive from her home in Los Angles every weekend to check on her mom and Jim. When Jim was finally discharged from the hospital, I came for a week to help Carol care for him. Once again, Carol found herself in the role of caregiver. A role that terrified her. A role she hated.

Unfortunately. Jim never fully recovered from these surgeries, partly because he continued to ignore his prescribed diet and exercise regimen. As the months went by, his condition slowly worsened. Jim began having episodes of congestive heart failure. These started with swelling in his ankles and legs, and eventually resulted in a buildup of fluid in his lungs. Jim would ignore these symptoms, refusing to see or even call his doctor until the fluid in his lungs left him struggling to breathe. At this point, Jim would panic and finally agree to let a terrified Carol call the paramedics. Because Jim waited so long to get medical treatment, he would end up spending several days in ICU before his doctors could stabilize his condition. Laura and Carol became frustrated by Jim's behavior. They knew that Jim's hospital stays could have been shorter or avoided altogether if only Jim had contacted his doctor when his symptoms first appeared.

Jim came home after each of his hospitalizations with a home health nurse checking on him every few days. While being seen by the nurse, Jim would follow his diet and do some mild exercise. But as soon as the nursing supervision stopped, Jim reverted back to his old lifestyle.

Laura called me after one of Jim's hospitalizations to update me on his latest medical crisis and to vent her frustration. Carol had called her daughter late one morning sounding absolutely frantic; Carol said Jim was very sick and refusing to see the doctor or to let her call the paramedics. Her mother wanted Laura to come right away.

The next several hours were filled with anxiety. Carol kept calling to see what time Laura thought she would arrive. Laura, who found herself stuck in LA traffic, kept reassuring her mother that she was coming as fast as traffic allowed. When Laura finally arrived four hours later, she found Jim sitting in his recliner, gasping for breath. Laura took one look at him and felt suddenly furious. Her tone was angry when she said, "Look at you, Pops. You're weak and you can barely breathe. You obviously need help. I don't know why on earth you haven't called the paramedics, but I'm calling them now." Jim shook his head, "No." "I have to call them Pops," Laura replied firmly. "You need help and mom is scared out of her wits. I don't care what you say, I'm calling them."

"Go ahead," Jim said defiantly, "You go ahead and call them but I'm not letting them in the house."

"So, I take it you've decided to just sit there and die," Carol replied angrily. "Well, you need help so I'm either calling the paramedics or hospice. Your choice. Which one do I call?"

Jim looked shocked at these words as though he suddenly became aware of the seriousness of his situation. "I guess you better call the paramedics," Jim gasped hanging his head in defeat. "I guess I don't have a choice. But God I hate going back to the hospital."

"I know how much Pops hates going to the hospital, that's why he puts off getting help," Laura said as she related the story to me. "But I can't understand why mom doesn't just ignore what Pops says and call 911 when he gets bad. It's hard for me to drop everything and come running every time Pops gets into trouble." It was obvious Jim's illness was taking a toll on Laura as she struggled to juggle work, family and caring for her mother and stepfather.

Over the following months, Jim grew steadily weaker and more fragile as his heart condition worsened. His feet and legs were constantly swollen now, and he had developed open sores on his legs which were difficult to heal. A nurse began visiting almost daily to assess his condition and change his bandaged legs. Jim was miserable and depressed. Because moving was such an effort, he rarely left home.

The final stage of Jim's illness began when he developed back pain. Instead of contacting his doctor about his pain, Jim decided to treat it himself and started taking ibuprofen. It did not take long for him to get into serious trouble. One morning several days later, Carol walked into the living room and found Jim sitting in his recliner, too weak to stand. He was shivering and deathly pale. For once Jim offered no resistance when Carol suggested calling the paramedics. Upon his arrival at the hospital, the doctors discovered Jim had developed severe GI bleeding from the combination of the ibuprofen and his blood thinner. It took ten units of blood to stabilize his condition before surgery could be done to stop the bleeding. This time Jim spent several weeks in ICU. When Jim was ready to be discharged, Carol asked Dr. Nelson to admit her husband to the nearby care center for some much-needed physical therapy. Jim weighed 240 pounds, and Carol worried she could not handle her husband at home in his weakened condition. Jim was tired of hospitals and pleaded with Dr. Nelson to just let him go home. Over Carol's objections, Dr. Nelson granted Jim's request. What neither of the men had considered when making this decision, was the fact that Jim had to walk up a flight of stairs to get into his house.

Laura arrived at the hospital to find Jim waiting, eager to leave. A nurse wheeled Jim to Laura's car and the two of them helped a shaky Jim get into the front seat. When they arrived at the couple's house, the trio suddenly realized that somehow Jim had to make it up the stairs. Carol ran to get a neighbor to help. Despite their efforts, Jim only managed to get halfway up the stairs before his knees buckled and he began falling backward. Luckily Laura, who was directly behind her stepfather, somehow managed to ease Pops to the ground. Carol ran and got a pillow to put under his head. Since the trio could not get Jim up by themselves, they had no choice but to call the paramedics. Jim laid helpless on the sidewalk waiting for their arrival. One look at Jim and the paramedics carefully loaded him on a stretcher and headed back to the hospital. Later, when Dr. Nelson saw Carol in the Emergency Department, he apologized saying, "I really should have listened to you about sending Jim home. You know him better than anyone. Next time, I promise I will do whatever you think is best." After a night in the hospital for observation, Jim, made no protest when he was discharged to the care center the next day.

Jim spent a month in center getting physical therapy and regaining some of his strength. When the doctor decided Jim was strong enough to go home, Carol, remembering their last fiasco, demanded to see Jim go up and down a flight of stairs before she would agree to take him home. Fortunately, Jim was able to pass her test.

I arrived the day before Jim's discharge to spend a week with the couple and help Carol with her husband's care. Once Jim was home, Carol seemed to assume if Jim was strong enough to come home, he was strong enough to take care of himself. She became angry when Jim said he was too weak to get his own breakfast, set up his medications, shower and shave by himself or clean up his bathroom. She justified her behavior by saying, "The staff at the care center spoiled him. They waited on him hand and foot. He didn't do anything for himself. Now he expects me to do the same. Well I just won't do it. There's no reason he can't do things for himself."

Her attitude left me speechless. This didn't sound like the Carol I knew. To me it was obvious that Jim was still very weak and needed help. Why didn't Carol see this? Then I realized how frightened she was. Carol did not want to admit Jim's physical condition was deteriorating because she was afraid of losing him. For her, it was easier to blame his weakened condition on laziness rather than face the fact he was steadily getting weaker.

As Jim and I sat talking one day, he began discussing his situation. "I know I am not going to get any better," he said. "And I don't want to go back to the hospital. I hate it there. I wish I could just stay at home."

I looked at Jim and said, "If you truly don't want to go back to the hospital, maybe you should talk to Dr. Nelson about hospice. Their nurses are real experts when it comes to finding ways to keep you comfortable at home whenever you start having problems." Jim became tearful at the mention of hospice, realizing I was affirming what he already suspected, he was dying. Seeing his tears, I walked over and gave him a hug saying, "I am so sorry. I know this is hard to think about." He nodded and made an effort to control his tears.

At the mention of hospice, Carol, who had been sitting listening to our conversation, spoke up saying angrily, "Don't be silly, Jim doesn't need hospice. How many times has he's been sick like this before? He always gets better. He just needs to stop expecting everyone to wait on him and start moving around so he gets his strength back." Despite the evidence, Carol clung to the belief that Jim would somehow manage to recover, and their life would return to normal. She was simply not ready to face the reality of their situation. Without Carol's support, I knew Jim would not agree to hospice.

Laura was very disappointed when I told her the couple refused to consider hospice. We both knew Jim was dying and found ourselves struggling to accept their decision. I wondered where Carol was going to find the emotional strength to handle yet another loss.

During the following months, Jim's symptoms continued to worsen. He was finding it harder to breathe despite using oxygen, his legs and feet were constantly swollen, and his kidneys were beginning to fail. He was miserable.

Several months later, Laura called to let me know Jim was back at the care center. He had fallen once again and been taken to the ER. When Laura arrived and saw how weak her stepfather had become, Laura knew it would be impossible for her mother to care for him at home.

She contacted Dr. Nelson and requested that Jim be sent to the care center and also be admitted to hospice. Surprisingly, the couple agreed to the plan. Laura told me the hospice nurse had my number and would call me later to update me on Jim's condition.

The hospice nurse, Sharon Steward, called me later that day. "We are giving Jim medication to ease his breathing and he seems comfortable," she reported. "He's sleeping a great deal of the time," she continued. "I don't think he's going to last more than a few days."

When I asked how Carol was doing, Sharon replied, "I know Carol is struggling, I understand this is the second husband she has lost. Our bereavement counselor saw Carol this afternoon and Carol seemed a little calmer after her visit. I just wish we had gotten the couple sooner. There is so much we could have done to help make this easier on the two of them. " "Believe me," I said, "Everyone tried to get them into hospice months ago. But Carol wouldn't even consider it. She refused to believe Jim wasn't going to recover."

That night, Carol was exhausted and desperately needed to go home but she hesitated to leave Jim by himself overnight. During the day he had become restless and kept trying to climb over the rails and get out of bed. Carol was afraid if he was left alone, he'd fall and hurt himself. Rita, a friend of Carol's. offered to spend the night sitting with Jim so Carol could get some sleep.

Later Rita told us that while she had been sitting reading her book, Jim had suddenly awakened. He looked at Rita and asked where Carol was. Rita said, "I told him Carol had gone home." Jim looked at Rita for a minute and then said, "That's too bad. I wanted to tell her goodbye," then closed his eyes and drifted back to sleep. Jim died later that night.

Carol called the next morning to tell me Jim was gone. "I am so sorry Carol," I said when I heard her news. "How are you doing? Are you all right?" I was surprised when Carol replied, "I'm actually doing really well. I had the most amazing experience. I woke up about midnight and looked around half asleep. Suddenly, I noticed three gold balls circling around the ceiling. They were just beautiful. As I lay there watching them, this feeling of peace came over me. Somehow, I knew Jim had just died and this was his way of saying goodbye to me. I drifted back to sleep and a few minutes later, the nurse called to tell me Jim had passed. When I went to see him and say goodbye, he had the most peaceful look on his face. I'm so glad he is finally out of pain."

When I arrived at Carol's the next day, I found in Carol, a mixture of sadness and peace. She repeated the story of the golden balls to everyone who came to see her and seemed to draw a special kind of strength from repeating the story. I stayed with Carol for several days while we began doing some of the immediate tasks that needed to be done following a death. Writing Jim's obituary, notifying relatives, returning medical equipment, changing names on bank accounts, contacting Social Security- the tasks seemed endless. At the end of the week, Laura arrived to bring her mother to Los Angles for a visit. Several weeks later, the family held a small memorial service for Jim in Laura's backyard. Afterwards Carol, with Laura's help, spread Jim's ashes in the canyon above the couple's home as Jim had requested.

The following year was an emotionally difficult one for Carol. Although she missed Jim terribly, Carol had spent most of her time the last several years caring for him. As her husband became too sick to leave home, Carol, afraid to leave Jim alone, became housebound too. During those years, Carol lived in a state of anxiety, never knowing when Jim might have another life-threatening episode. Now Carol felt guilty about the overwhelming sense of relief she was feeling that the ordeal was finally over. Feeling relieved in Carol's mind was not the way you mourned the loss of your husband.

Sensing her mother's emotional distress, Laura encouraged Carol to attend a bereavement group sponsored by the hospice that had cared for Jim. During one of their meetings, Carol shared her bewildering mixture of feelings. Much to her surprise, Carol found many long-time caregivers had felt that same relief when their spouses died. As Carol began to realize her feelings were a normal response to what she had experienced, her guilt started to dissipate.

A year after Jim's death, Carol decided to sell her mobile home and move to LA to be closer to her family. She is enjoying being near her daughter and watching her great-grandchildren grow up. Carol and I continue to be close friends and we still manage to get together several times a year.

Afterthoughts

Because of my background in hospice, I found it extremely frustrating to witness the final stage of Jim's illness. During my visits, I worked hard to suppress my urge to somehow bully the couple into accepting hospice care. Although intellectually I accepted the fact that Jim and Carol had the right to decide not to enter hospice, emotionally I was saddened by the fact that I knew this decision prevented them from making the most of the time Jim had left. Jim spent much of his last few months ping-ponging between home, the hospital and the care center. Hospice nurses, with their end-of-life expertise would have found ways to manage Jim's breathlessness at home, making his many panicky trips to the hospital no longer necessary. Carol, who struggled with her feelings of anxiety and anger throughout Jim's illness, could have benefited from the emotional comfort and support the hospice nurses and counselors would have provided. Knowing this, whenever I visited the couple, I found myself remembering a difficult lesson I learned during my years of nursing; never want more for someone than they wanted for themselves. Refusing hospice until the very end was Jim's and Carol's choice. One they had a right to make. My job was to support their choice by giving them whatever help they were willing to accept.

EMMA MATTHEWS

Families often find it difficult to communicate their feelings to a dying loved one.

When I was working as a hospice nurse, I found there were certain families I felt a connection with the moment I met them. I mentally thought of such families as "my carrots" and looked forward to my visits with them, especially when I was having a rough day. These families had similar characteristics. The members were warm and loving towards one another and made anyone who walked through their door feel a part of the family. These individuals were resilient, supportive and somehow able to maintain a sense of humor in the direst of circumstances. I was filled with admiration for the way they coped with their various situations and learned so much from working with them. Looking back, I think one of my very favorite "carrot" families was the Matthews.

Emma Matthews, a tiny 85-year-old woman, arrived on our Hospice In-patient Unit several months after being diagnosed with ovarian cancer. During the months prior to her admission, Emma's pain had steadily worsened despite her physician's efforts to control it. Desperate to find something, anything, to relieve Emma's suffering, her doctor consulted our hospice medical director, Dr. Long, knowing he was an expert in pain control. Dr. Long recommended Emma be admitted to the inpatient unit so the effectiveness of the medications he wanted to try could be closely monitored by him and the nursing staff.

Although Emma realized why her admission was necessary, she was not happy about her inpatient stay. She hated hospitals, missed her home, her cat, her garden and being among her own things. At first Emma was withdrawn and somewhat cold and distant to the nurses. But as her pain gradually subsided, Emma's sense of humor and spunky personality began to emerge. She soon became a favorite with the staff who appreciated her quick wit and independent spirit.

Emma had three daughters: Susan and Karen, who lived near their mother, and Becky who had traveled from her home in the Midwest to help her sisters with their mother's care. Emma's husband had died in his early thirties, leaving his wife to raise their three daughters alone. Because of the family's struggles both emotionally and financially, Emma and her daughters were unusually close.

Knowing how Emma hated being away from home, her daughters focused their energy on making Emma's room as cozy as possible. Pictures of Emma's family were placed by her bedside and the girls decorated the walls with cards from friends and pictures drawn by Emma's grandchildren. Bouquets of fresh flowers from Emma's garden stood in vases around the room. Favorite foods were brought in and the four Matthews often ate meals together in Emma's room or out on the adjoining patio. Occasionally, one of the girls would bring along Emma's cat for a visit. As soon as Sulky saw Emma, he would begin purring so loudly he could be heard by visitors in the hallway. This was his way of letting everyone know how much he missed his mistress and how glad he was to see her.

During her hospice stay, Emma continually complained of feeling chilly despite the extra blankets the nurses brought her. Finally, Susan brought Emma a fluffy blue blanket from home which Emma promptly wrapped over her head and around her shoulders, with only her tiny wrinkled little face peeking out between the blanket edges. When her nurse saw Emma sitting in a chair snuggled up in her blanket, she burst out laughing. Telling, telling Emma, she looked just like a little ET. Much to Emma's delight, the nickname stuck, and she became ET to all the hospice staff from then on. She loved it.

I met the Matthews family several days after Emma's admission. I was the nurse who would be visiting Emma at home and wanted to take the opportunity to meet Emma and her daughters before Emma was discharged. I arrived on the inpatient unit early one morning and introduced myself. Emma looked me up and down and said with an expressionless face, "Are you sure you want to be my nurse? I'm not always easy to get along with and I don't follow orders very well."

"I heard." I replied. "The in-patient staff warned us about you. When the homecare crew heard you were being discharged, we met to see which one of us was going to get stuck with seeing you. Unfortunately, I drew the short straw." Emma burst out laughing. "You and I are going to get along just fine," she said. "I just needed to make sure I wasn't getting some nurse with a stick up her backside."

A week after her admission, Emma's pain was well controlled, and preparations began for her discharge home. A hospital bed was delivered to her house, along with a walker and bedside commode. The daughters received instructions on Emma's medications and the care she would need at home. Everything was in place for Emma to leave the inpatient unit the following morning. I planned to visit that afternoon to check in with the family and see how things were going.

I received a phone call early the next morning from an inpatient nurse telling me a visit to the Matthews that day would not be necessary. Emma had slipped into a coma during the night and would not be going home. It appeared Emma had reached the final stage of her illness. Her daughters, who were devastated, kept a tearful, round-the-clock vigil at her bedside. I stopped by several times to see how they were doing and to offer my support. "We're hanging in there," Susan said, the first time I visited. "We keep saying we think mom planned it this way because she didn't trust us to take care of her," Karen added. "She kept saying she didn't want to be a burden, she just hated having to ask us to do things for her. She insisted on being as independent as possible." Whether or not it was Emma's plan to spare her daughters caregiving chores, it seemed there was nothing left for anyone to do but wait.

You can't imagine how shocked I was when the inpatient staff contacted me several days later to tell me Emma had unexpectedly regained consciousness. She was sitting up in bed, visiting with her daughters and demanding ice cream. When I arrived at the hospice unit later that day,

Susan rushed out of Emma's room, gave me a hug and said, "Can you believe it? Mom's wide awake." And Susan began telling me what had happened.

Just before dawn that morning, Karen and Becky went to take a nap in the inpatient family room while Susan sat by Emma's bedside. Suddenly, Susan said, she became aware that her mother's eyes were open, and Emma was looking right at her. "I was shocked. I couldn't believe what I was seeing," Susan said. "I jumped up and leaned over the bed to get a closer look. It took a minute for it to sink in, mom was really awake. I asked mom how she was feeling, and she said, 'Hungry!'" Susan looked at her mother and shook her head. "The next minute I was running down the hall to tell the nurses and to get my sisters," Susan continued. "No one would believe me until they saw her with their own eyes."

I looked at Emma who was lying in bed looking amused as she listened to Susan's story. "Well Emma, welcome back." I said. "You really had us going." Emma gave me a mischievous grin as though she had played a deliberate joke on all of us.

News that Emma had pulled a "Lazarus" quickly spread among the hospice staff. A "Lazarus" is an expression used among hospice workers to describe a situation where someone who appears to be on the verge of dying any minute suddenly regains consciousness and goes on to live a few more days, weeks or even months. We all agreed if anyone would pull a "Lazarus" it would be Emma, our tricky little ET.

Several days passed and Emma, though weak, had no recurrence of her coma. Her pain remained well controlled with the new medication. Seeing how well she was doing, her daughters asked if they could take their mother home. Dr. Long agreed there was nothing more the inpatient team could do for Emma and once again plans were made for Emma's discharge. She was ecstatic at the thought of going home.

Emma left the hospice unit the next morning. The transition home went very smoothly. When I arrived at the Matthews that afternoon, Emma was settled into a hospital bed which had been set up in her living room, close to a window where she could look out on her garden. Emma's three daughters quickly learned how to provide the physical care their mother needed and seemed to derive a special satisfaction from caring for the mother who had given so much to them. As the days passed, the three focused their attention on inventing ways to keep their Mom comfortable and entertained.

One of the first challenges Emma's daughters faced was finding ways to encourage their mother to eat. The girls spent hours fixing all Emma's favorite foods, but when a meal was placed in front of her, Emma would pick at the food, only eating a bite or two. Although intellectually the girls understood Emma's loss of appetite was due to her illness, emotionally, they found it distressing to see their mother not eating. The three felt neglectful if they couldn't coax Emma to "just take a few more bites," and they became determined to find a way to encourage Emma to eat. After several failed plans, the girls finally hit upon a strategy that worked. Knowing how much their Mom loved to play poker, the girls agreed to play one hand of poker with Emma for every bite of food she ate. Much to their delight, Emma began eating small portions of food several times a day.

Although very weak, Emma's mischievous nature remained intact. One morning when I dropped by, Susan answered the door saying with a grin, "Just wait until you hear Mom's latest." "What have you been up to now Emma?" I asked as I entered the room. All eyes were on Emma and everyone began laughing. Susan turned to me and began to explain. "As you know, Mom and the three of us have been having a major battle about whether or not she needs one of us to sleep in her room at night. We just don't feel comfortable leaving her alone. She is so stubborn; she refuses to call us if she needs to get up and we are afraid she'll fall. So, we laid down the law. We've insisted on taking turns sleeping on the couch by her bed."

"I don't need anyone with me," Emma protested. giving her girls a disgruntled look. "All night long the girls keep coming and checking on me to see if I'm still breathing. It's unnerving to wake up from a sound sleep

117

and see one of them hanging over the bed, looking down at me. It startles me every time it happens. I keep telling them I'd sleep much better if they just slept in their own beds and let me be."

"Since we refused to listen to her," Karen continued, "She decided to teach us a lesson." Last night was Karen's turn to sleep in her mother's room. Emma laid in wait and when she heard Karen tiptoeing over to check on her, Emma laid perfectly still with her eyes closed and held her breath. What started out as a routine check on her mother suddenly became a moment of panic when Karen realized her mother wasn't breathing. Karen, thinking her mother had died, ran and woke her sisters.

"When Karen told us, we ran to mom's room," Susan said. "The first thing I did was put my hand on mom's chest to see if I could feel any movement. I felt nothing, her chest was perfectly still. We were sure she was dead. We just stood there, wondering what to do next. Suddenly mom opened her eyes and shouted, "Boo." "We must have jumped six feet," Becky laughed, shaking her head at her mother. "She scared us to death."

"Serves you right, the way you three hover over me like a bunch of vultures, waiting for something to happen," Emma grumbled. "Tonight, I would appreciate it if you girls would just go sleep in your own beds and leave me alone. When something happens, it's going to happen whether you are with me or not."

Clearly, this had become a major issue. Searching for an acceptable compromise, I suggested the family purchase a set of baby monitors and place one in Emma's room and one in the girls. This way Emma's daughters could hear Emma if she called out or tried to get up and it would still allow Emma her privacy at night. After some rather heated discussion around the issue of whether Emma really needed monitoring, everyone finally agreed to the plan and nights became more restful at the Matthews' household.

This was not the last time Emma and her daughters locked horns. One morning when I arrived for a visit, I found Emma and the girls arguing over whether Emma should start walking daily to and from the mailbox. The girls were insisting Emma needed to get some exercise to regain her strength and Emma was flatly refusing to cooperate. "Mom hardly moves at all," Becky said turning to me, hoping to enlist my support. "It's no wonder she's getting weaker. I would too if I just sat around all day." I glanced at Emma and saw she was glaring at Becky and stubbornly shaking her head no. "I am not going to do it," Emma declared. "No matter what any of you say, I'm not going to do it." "But Mom," Becky began in a pleading tone. "No," Emma said sharply cutting Becky off mid-sentence, "I know you girls mean well but if anyone says another word about exercising, I am going to ask you to leave. I am not going to tell you again."

"Don't you think Mom should do something besides just sit around?" Becky asked me, ignoring her mother's comment. I felt all eyes turn towards me, waiting for my answer. "When someone has an incurable condition," I began cautiously, "It is very difficult for the people who love them to accept that there is nothing they can do to make that person stronger. When your mother refuses to exercise, or to eat the way you think she should, it is easy to feel she is just 'giving up', not putting up a fight, not trying. Often this makes us feel angry. You are right, your mother is growing weaker, but her weakness isn't because she's not exercising, it's because the cancer is steadily growing, and this growth is taking all her energy and strength. I know the three of you want to do everything possible to help your mother, but the truth is there is nothing more you or anyone else can do to make your mother stronger."

The girls' eyes filled with tears as they listened. "Sometimes it helps to think of energy as though it is money in a bank account," I continued. "The amount of energy your Mom has in her account each day is very limited and she needs to spend it wisely. Doesn't it make more sense for her to spend her energy on activities she enjoys rather than insisting she spend it exercising? A walk to and from the mailbox would totally drain her account and she wouldn't have any energy left to do the kind of things she likes."

Emma had been nodding her head in agreement while I was talking, but her daughters were struggling with the implication of what I was saying. This discussion had brought the girls a step closer to facing the reality that they had no control over their mother's condition and what would happen next; a situation that is difficult for most of us to handle. Gradually, as the girls began to accept the reality of their mother's condition, they were able to promise their mother there would be no more mention of exercise.

I suggested to the girls that they let Emma decided how she wanted to spend her days and how much activity she could tolerate. The girls agreed this was a good idea. Emma gave a sigh of relief.

Life in the Matthews' household settled into a comfortable routine after this. The girls began asking Emma what she would like to do that day, often pushing her wheelchair into the garden where Emma liked to sit in the sun and enjoy her flowers or they arranged visits with friends. But it was obvious to everyone that Emma was slowly fading. She tired more easily, and she was becoming more withdrawn, preferring quiet to the chatter of people. Her daughters began limiting the number of visitors saying, "Mom isn't up to much company right now." Those who were allowed to see her were told not to stay long.

One day when I stopped by, I was greeted by a tearful Susan who said, "I am so glad you're here. I don't know what is going on with mother. She's been biting our heads off all morning, complaining about everything. When we ask her what's wrong, she just looks at us and shakes her head. Maybe you can find out what's bothering her." Normally at least one of the girls was present when I visited with Emma, but this time I suggested I talk to Emma alone.

I walked into the room and approached Emma's bed saying, "I hear you are having a rough day Emma, what's going on? Are you having pain?" "No, no pain," Emma snapped. "What is it then Emma? How can I help?"

Emma gave me a long, gauging look and said somewhat reluctantly, "It's my girls. I just don't know what is going on with them. I feel like they don't care that I'm dying." Much to my astonishment, a tear rolled down her cheek. "Help me understand why you feel they don't care," I said gently, taking Emma's hand.

"I'm dying, and those girls go around acting like we are having one big party, laughing and joking all the time. I haven't seen one of them so much as shed a tear. Don't they feel bad about what is happening to me? Don't they realize I don't have much time left? There are things I want to say to them but every time I try to have a serious talk with them, they just change the subject or tell me to stop being morbid."

"Oh Emma," I said, giving her hand a squeeze. "Your girls love you very much. They are just trying to keep up a brave face in front of you. When I am here, they may laugh and joke while we are with you but the minute, we step out of your room they begin crying." Emma gave me a skeptical look. "Let me talk to them and encourage them to share their feelings with you."

Emma's daughters were hovering around the doorway when I came out. I suggested the four of us go to the kitchen and sit down for a talk. "Did you find out what's wrong with mom," Susan asked anxiously. "Why she's so upset?" I shared what Emma had told me. The girls were stunned. Then Becky said, "We were afraid if we started telling mom how sad we are and how much we are going to miss her, we would start crying and it would make her feel bad."

"She has enough to deal with having the cancer without worrying about us," Karen added. "Looks like we need to have a talk with Mom and straighten things out," Susan said. "But how do you start a conversation like that? You can't just say, 'I wish you didn't have to die Mom.'"

"I know it's hard to talk about these things," I said. "People are always afraid of saying the wrong thing. But you could begin by telling your mom how sad you are that she is having to go through this illness," I suggested. "Share how much you love having her for a mother- the

121

things you will never forget about her- the things you enjoyed doing with her- the ways you are going to miss her. Let her know that although you will miss her like crazy, it's okay for her to go whenever she's ready. You three will take care of each other. You will be okay." With these suggestions in mind, the girls were finally able to talk about their feelings of sadness and grief with Emma. The Matthews spent that afternoon sharing tears and hugs, followed by periods of teasing and laughter as the four recalled their favorite memories. It was a healing time for everyone.

As the days slipped by, Emma grew impatient to just "get on with things." During each visit she insisted I check her blood pressure and listen to her heart and lungs. As I moved my stethoscope across her chest listening, I could feel her anxiously searching my face for some sign that things were changing. "Is my blood pressure still good?" she would ask and then look disappointed when I reported no change. "I don't understand it," she would say. "How much longer can this go on?"

"I wish I knew Emma," I replied, the first time she asked me this question. "With some people, this stage can last a few weeks and for others, things change suddenly, and they are gone." I knew these were not the words she wanted to hear. I just sat with her for a few minutes gently patting her hand. This was the only comfort I could give her.

Emma's lingering also weighed heavily on her daughters. Originally, the girls had expected to be with their mother for a few weeks, but they were now in their third month of caregiving. Their families missed them and wanted them home. Karen, who was scheduled to go to Hawaii with her husband in two weeks, began wondering if she should she cancel her trip. Becky was concerned she would not be home in time for her son's high school graduation. Although they were aware their mother was miserable and wanted things to be over, the trio still felt guilty about finding themselves wondering how soon her death might occur. They knew their mother would understand if they needed to get back to their families, but not being with Emma at the end was an option they were unwilling to consider.

The following week, rapid changes in Emma's condition began to occur and she appeared to be in the final stages of dying. She refused all food, preferring ice chips or sips of water. She became much less alert, drifting in and out of consciousness. Karen reported Emma had asked to have a picture of her husband placed near her bedside where she could see it. As the dying process progressed, Emma began to withdraw completely. refusing not only to interact with friends but also with her daughters. She avoided talking to her girls whenever possible, often turning her back to her daughters, pretending to be asleep when they tried to converse with her. This left the trio feeling their mother was rejecting them just when they wanted to feel close to her, knowing there was not much time left. The girls were confused, unable to understand what was happening.

I explained that often people, at the very end, shut down and disconnect from everyone they love so they can concentrate their energy on their final task- leaving. "Your mom isn't rejecting you," I reassured the girls. "Because the bond between the four of you is so strong, your mom has to disconnect emotionally from you in order to gather the strength to go and leave you three behind. This is what is happening now. She is detaching emotionally so she can take the next step- so she can leave."

During this visit, we talked about what changes in care their mother would need during this final stage. I reminded the trio there was a hospice nurse available at any time day or night if they felt they needed additional help or support. The women said they felt confident they could handle this final stage but would call if there were any problems.

Susan called me about eight o'clock the following morning to tell me their mother's breathing had become quite irregular and she thought Emma was nearing the end. When I arrived, I found Emma surrounded by her daughters. The girls were sitting by their mother's bed, holding her hands. As I stood watching, Emma's eyes briefly opened, and she gave us a weak smile. Soon her breathing stopped, and she was gone. The room suddenly became very still, then filled with a peaceful silence.

Emma's daughters sat and held their mother for a few more minutes, quietly saying their goodbyes.

Afterwards, we sat in the kitchen and had a cup of tea together while the girls talked about Emma and what they had just experienced. "It seems like mother's dying just went on and on and that it would never be over," Becky said as we sat sipping our tea. "But I think we needed the extra time," Becky continued. "We needed to see how much being here with us was costing her physically and emotionally. Seeing that made it easier for us to let her go." Her two sisters nodded in agreement. Although sad about their mother's death, the women were also relieved their mother was finally at peace. The trio found comfort from the knowledge that they had fulfilled their mother's final wish, to die in her own home.

I saw the girls for the last time several days later at Emma's funeral. After the other guests had gone the four of us stood talking, laughing and reminiscing about our experiences together. When it was time for me to leave, I became teary as I hugged each daughter and said my goodbyes. Working with these strong, loving, feisty young women had been an amazing experience, one I will never forget.

Afterthoughts

Working with the Matthews increased my awareness of just how difficult it is for families to change the focus of their care. Encouraging the ailing person to eat more food or to exercise is often an attempt by the family to feel they are doing everything possible for their loved one.

Towards the end of their illness, most people stop eating and eventually will also stop drinking. As the person grows weaker, their body no longer produces the enzymes needed to digest food. When this happens, food that is eaten lies undigested causing discomfort. Our bodies seem to understand this, and the dying individual instinctively stops eating.

A similar thing happens with liquids. As the heart grows weaker, it is no longer able to pump fluid throughout the body. Excess fluid ends up lodging in the lungs, making it difficult for the person to breathe. When someone stops drinking, families may wonder if IV fluids should be given. Starting someone on IV fluids at this final stage causes severe breathing problems because of the buildup of fluid in the lungs and most physicians avoid doing this. The body knows what it needs to do to make dying as comfortable as possible. It is important, I feel, for family members to aware of this process so they know not to ask for medical interventions which could interfere with this process.

Changing the focus of their activities from health promotion to comfort care requires a major shift in thinking for most individuals. When family members are able to make this shift and accept the reality that their love one is dying, they can move into a new phase of caregiving. One focused on providing physical comfort, saying goodbyes, offering emotional support and making the most of the time that is left.

The Matthews also helped me to understand how painful it is for families when their loved one emotionally withdraws as he or she nears the end. This is a time when those close to the dying individual sense the person is about to leave them and their natural instinct is to want to engage that person and feel emotionally close to them for as long as possible. When the dying person doesn't respond to their efforts to connect, this unresponsiveness often feels like rejection to those who are being left behind unless they understand that this withdrawal is a normal part of dying.

HOSPICE

Hospice is the most comprehensive medical benefit ever enacted.

The wife of a terminally ill man once told me, "Calling hospice was the hardest phone call I've ever made." It is a phone call many people put off making, despite the fact that the cost of six months of hospice care for terminally ill people is covered by most private insurances, Medicaid and Medicare. The average hospice patient receives just twenty-two days of care, a fraction of the amount of care he or she is entitled to receive. The reasons for this delay in enrolling in hospice are varied. Often, I have found, people put off contacting hospice because they believe hospice services should not be used until the patient's condition becomes "really bad." Other individuals are simply not emotionally ready to face the fact that they or someone they love is dying. In some instances, people don't know how to contact a hospice or don't realize they may be able to receive hospice services even if they have no medical insurance.

In my opinion, it is much easier for everyone involved when a terminally ill person enters hospice before reaching the final stages of his or her disease. I can't tell you how many times I have arrived at a home to admit someone to hospice and found the patient not eating, experiencing severe pain and/or nausea and too weak to get out of bed. Usually, in these cases, the family is in a state of panic, not knowing what to do or how to care for their loved one.

When an individual receives a terminal diagnosis, the person and those closest to him or her experience anxiety and fear– fear about what the future holds, together with doubts about their ability to cope with what lies ahead. Often these people feel isolated and alone. Much of this sense of isolation and fear dissipates when an individual begins receiving hospice care. Meeting the members of the hospice team gives patients and families a sense of relief, knowing they are no longer facing the death alone. Now they have end-of-life experts in place, ready to provide assistance. Having a nurse on call 24/7 to make a home visit

126

whenever needed gives the family an additional sense of security, knowing help is readily available should they need it.

When my dad suddenly became extremely anxious late one evening, I called the hospice nurse for help. After listening to my concerns, the nurse arranged to have a medication to relieve his anxiety delivered to our home in the middle of the night, a service I greatly appreciated at the time.

Hospices provide a variety of services. The most frequent hospice visitor is usually the nurse, who monitors the patient's condition, works closely with the physician to adjust medications as needed and teaches the caregivers how to make the dying individual comfortable. Home health aides are available to visit several times a week to help with personal care such as bathing and feeding. Trained volunteers can stay with the patient for several hours, allowing caregivers time away from home. Social workers provide emotional support, help find community resources and assist families in finalizing funeral arrangements, along with many other services. Chaplains, skilled in offering spiritual support, are also part of the hospice team, along with bereavement counselors who assist family members struggling with the issues of grief and loss. Terminally ill individuals and their families can choose which services they wish to receive.

Once a patient is admitted to a hospice program, the cost of medical equipment needed by the patient such as a wheelchair, a hospital bed, a shower chair or a commode is covered by the hospice. The hospice also pays for any medications that are related to the patient's condition and delivers them to the individual's home. There are no co-pays for medical equipment or medications when they are provided by hospice.

In addition to addressing the needs of dying individuals, hospice is also concerned with the needs of the family. How well are they coping with the illness? Do these family members need counseling? Extra emotional support? Spiritual care? Respite? What are the family's expectations of how the death will occur? How well do they understand the changes that are occurring in the patient's condition? By identifying and addressing the needs of both the patient and his or her family, the hospice team can help these individuals make the most of the time that is left.

People residing in skilled care facilities are also eligible for hospice. Nurses along with other hospice team members will visit these individuals regularly and provide the same types of services that are received by patients living at home. Translators are available to families when needed.

Although most hospice patients prefer to stay at home, there are situations when an individual may need to be admitted to an inpatient facility. These days many hospices do not have their own inpatient units. Instead, most hospices contract with a skilled nursing facility to provide beds for their hospice patients when needed. Someone is admitted for inpatient care when the family is unable to handle his or her death at home or if an individual is experiencing symptoms such as pain that can't be managed at home without undue stress on the family. The cost of an inpatient admission is entirely paid for by the hospice. It is part of the hospice benefit.

Anyone can make a referral to hospice: a doctor, a social worker, a patient, a family member or friend. Among the many diseases found among hospice patients are heart disease, COPD, renal disease, multiple sclerosis, ALS, and Parkinson's, as well as cancer. Individuals who have one of these diseases qualify to receive hospice care if they are progressing toward the end stage of their illness. Other individuals who may also be eligible for hospice are elderly men and women who have no diagnosed terminal illness but are becoming weak and frail— simply wearing out. The life expectancy of patients with dementia or who have suffered a stroke is more difficult to determine, and for this reason these individuals may have a more difficult time qualifying for hospice services.

Some guidelines about when to call hospice include:

1. When an individual is having frequent hospitalizations or Emergency Department visits and has decided he or she no longer wants to continue going to the hospital for treatment.
2. When an individual has been told by his or her doctor that there is nothing more that can be done to treat or cure the illness and the person is no longer seeking curative treatment.
3. When someone aged is becoming frail, weak, and is losing weight.
4. When an individual is experiencing unrelieved or poorly controlled symptoms such as pain or nausea and have declined in their ability to care for themselves.

Most urban areas have more than one hospice available to people who need hospice care. Unless your HMO or other medical provider is contracted with a particular hospice, individuals have a choice regarding which hospice they wish to use. Hospital social workers or physicians may recommend a hospice to you. If you find yourself in this situation, ask the person what their reason is for suggesting that particular hospice. Is it because they have first-hand knowledge of the quality of service provided by this hospice? Or is it because they were impressed with the marketing person who visited them?

According to the rules governing hospices, individuals have the right to interview several different hospices before choosing one. Some questions to ask when interviewing a hospice are:

1. Who provides their nursing care- RNs who are certified in palliative care or LVNs?
2. How often on average do the nurses and home health aides visit?
3. Do their social workers and chaplains hold master's degrees?
4. What facility do they use for their inpatient beds?
5. Can the hospice provide short-term 24-hour care in the home if needed?
6. Who comes on the initial visit, an RN or an admissions counselor?

In the end, many people follow their instincts and choose the hospice that feels right to them. Remember that under the hospice benefit, individuals never lose their right to choose. If, for whatever reason, a person finds they are unhappy with the hospice they have chosen, the individual maintains the right to choose a different one. If someone changes his or her mind and no longer wishes to receive hospice services, that individual is allowed disenroll from hospice altogether and reenter a hospice program at a later date. Occasionally, a patient or a family member finds they dislike or feel uncomfortable around a member of the hospice team who is caring for them. If this occurs, don't hesitate to call the hospice and ask them to send someone else. It is important to feel at ease with those who are coming to provide care.

Often when someone finds out I am a retired hospice nurse; they begin telling me their "hospice story." These individuals describe how much help hospice was when their mother or father, sister or brother was dying. Their story always ends the same way: 'Hospice was just wonderful. I don't know what we would have done without them." Sometimes the person adds, "I just wish we had called them sooner."

If you think you or any of your loved ones might be eligible to receive hospice care, I encourage you to talk to your doctor or call your local hospice. Hospices are always willing to come and assess your particular situation. Finding ways to deal with a terminal illness is difficult for both patients and their loved ones. At times the situation can feel overwhelming. Reach out for help. Hospices, with their expertise in end-of-life care, can help ease the stresses that come with the final chapter of a life.

ACKNOWLEDGMENTS

This book was written with the help of many people. The book began when I started writing about some of my experiences with people who were dying and reading these stories to the women in my AAUW writing group: Beth, Peggy, Margo, Donna, Susan, Elsa, Janet, Jean, Chris, Jenny, Nancy, Marsha, Inger, Suman and Anne. These wonderful women listened to my stories and encouraged me to publish them.

With the idea of publishing my book in mind, I contacted Arlene Carlson, a retired bereavement counselor I had worked with, and asked for her help editing my chapters. Since Arlene lives in Tucson AZ, and I in California, we did this mainly through telephone conferences, which sometimes lasted several hours. I so appreciate her help and input.

I also want to thank Tani Bhati, another former hospice colleague, who reviewed and edited my chapter on hospice services to make sure the content is accurate and up to date.

Once my book was nearing completion, I turned for help to my very talented niece Danielle Egnew, who walked me through the steps needed to publish my book on Amazon. Danielle also offered to draw the picture that appears on the cover of my book. Because she is a very talented artist, I gratefully accepted her offer.

Since I am terrible at punctuation, so I also enlisted the expertise of two friends, Laura Cline and Christine Hunt, who agreed to read through the manuscript and correct all my many punctuation errors. I learned a lot working with the two of them. Thank you both so much.

And lastly, I am very grateful to the individuals whose stories appear in the chapters of this book. Dying is a very sacred time in someone's life. It was a privilege to be allowed to be present and to witness the final chapter of each of their lives.

Photo by Susan Brazelton

I welcome questions and comments from readers. You can reach me at my website, joanstempel.com

Made in the USA
Lexington, KY
20 November 2019